Spade, Skirret
and Parsnip

Spade, Skirret and Parsnip

The CURIOUS History of VEGETABLES

BILL LAWS

FOREWORD BY HENRIETTA GREEN

SUTTON PUBLISHING

First published in 2004 by
Sutton Publishing Limited · Phoenix Mill
Thrupp · Stroud · Gloucestershire · GL5 2BU

British Library Cataloguing in Publication Data
A catalogue record for this book is available from the British
Library.

ISBN 0-7509-3258-9

Typeset in 11/14pt Photina.
Typesetting and origination by
Sutton Publishing Limited.
Printed and bound in England by
J.H. Haynes & Co. Ltd, Sparkford.

Contents

Acknowledgements

I am grateful to Howard and Peggy Laws for nurturing the gardener in me and to Geoff and Pauline Martin for entrusting their vegetable patch in Brighton to me back in the 1970s. For other material I am indebted to staff at the Royal Horticultural Society library, especially Jennifer Vine and Dr Brent Elliott; to staff at the Henry Doubleday Research Association, the National Trust, English Heritage, National Society of Allotments and Leisure Gardeners, The Museum of Garden History, Sutton Consumer Products and Darren Rowe, the Ruskin Foundation, Pilsbury Company, Neil Porteous of Clumber Park, Weald and Downland Open Air Museum, Kew Gardens, the Musée des Johnnies, Roscoff, Birds Eye Foods and Bea Slizewski and Floriade in the Netherlands; vegetable gardeners at Hunger Hill, Nottingham, and allotment-holders Jude Cooper, Sue Oliver and Gabriel Jackson and walled gardener David Petts; the villagers of Bucknell and the Watkins family; Sandy Green for making free with her garden and library; Julie Lachaud for her French translations; Medwyn Williams of Anglesey; Ray Warner of Thomas Etty Esq., Heritage Seeds; and Debbie Rees at Hampton Court. The extract from the poem on p. 58 is reprinted with permission from A.P. Watt Ltd on behalf of Michael B. Yeats. I am also indebted to my agent, Chelsey Fox, and to the editorial skills of Jaqueline Mitchell and Hilary Walford. Thanks too to Liz Andrews, Chris Bauer, Bobbie Blackwell, Hugh Bryant, Alison Chapman, Fiona Grant, Gillian Linscott, Eileen Klotz, Michelle Seddon-Harvey, Paul and Vicki Murray, Carole Protherough, Trevor Reed, Keith and Doreen Ruck and Glen Storhaug. I am obliged as ever to Sarah, Kahlia and Rosie and especially to Abby, to whom this book is dedicated. All photographs are by the author unless credited otherwise.

Foreword

Vegetable gardening came comparatively late into my life. If truth be told, no gardening – vegetables or otherwise – figured until, in pursuit of the rural idyll, I moved to Gloucestershire.

London was where I misspent my childhood. Blessed with a large garden, I whiled away hour after hour playing with my Scottie dog Kim or, later on, flirting with my next-door neighbour while he fed his chickens – and yes, he did keep hens and an excessively cock-a-doodling cock in the poshest part of St John's Wood. Gardening was something done by a stream of gardeners.

Even though I never once saw my mother cook a meal, I have enjoyed a happy career as a food writer. Equally, even though I never saw either of my parents wield so much as a pair of secateurs, it has not prevented me from embracing gardening with all the passion of a late convert.

In *Spade, Skirret and Parsnip*, Bill Laws makes me realise what a fascinating pastime I have latterly adopted. With all its irritations, foibles, triumphs and disappointments, gardening mirrors life. Vegetables were the staff of life and, just as snobbery existed in the world at large, so it did in the kitchen garden. Imagine the pressure on the 'gentleman's gardener' who not only had to grow the right vegetables but had to get them to the table at the right time, preferably long before 'poor people even think of such a thing'.

By celebrating our history of vegetables, Bill Laws highlights the facts and foibles for our pleasure and edification. He certainly – if you will forgive the pun – knows his onions. *Spade, Skirret and*

Parsnip is a charming read, written with authority, a gentle humour and a superb feel for detail. So next time you get your spade from the shed to dig 'the plot', you may be reassured to know that you are merely one in a long line of vegetable fanatics.

Henrietta Green

Introduction

From painters and rock stars to politicians and poets, people have taken their vegetables very seriously.

There was the Suffolk clergyman who was convinced that growing vegetables reduced street crime and the garden correspondent who claimed that writers who ate potatoes became verbose. There was the American president Woodrow Wilson, who told his people that raising vegetables would cure them of their 'extravagant and wasteful' ways, and the Victorian critic John Ruskin, who believed that growing vegetables would better your position in society and probably improve your table manners.

Monet would break away from painting the water lilies at Giverny only to check the progress of his kitchen garden next door. And some historians are convinced that the Roman Empire would have survived longer had its emperor Diocletian remained at his post in Rome instead of taking early retirement to grow cabbages at his Illyrian palace. 'Could you but see the vegetables I have raised,' he enthused to a friend, even as the empire descended into civil war. Yet it was these conquering Italians who gave us the word 'vegetable' from *vegere*, to grow, to animate and to enliven. The vegetable has continued to fire enthusiasms ever since.

Some people have grown vegetables as a form of protest against a range of foes from wealthy landowners and multinationals to American military powers. Others, like the Protestants of northern Europe, once refused to have anything to do with the potato on

Instead . . .

We don't just say: eat more potatoes. We say: eat more potatoes *instead*. You see the point?

Careful planning, lucky weather, farmers and farm workers, subsidies and low fixed prices—these gave us a bumper potato crop.

HOME-GROWN FOOD! And delicious home-grown food it is, if you treat it right! Don't be content with just 'plain boiled' potatoes. It's cheap and it's easy to make many delicious dishes with them.

The **POTATO PLAN**

1 Serve potatoes for breakfast on three days a week.

2 Make your main dish a potato dish one day a week.

3 Refuse second helpings of other food until you've had more potatoes.

4 Serve potatoes in other ways than 'plain boiled.' Here's one to start on :

SCALLOPED POTATOES

Ingredients : 2 lb. potatoes, 1 tablespoonful flour, ½ pint household milk, 1 tablespoonful chopped onion, 4 oz. grated cheese, 2 tablespoonfuls chopped parsley, salt, pepper. *Method :* Scrub potatoes, cut into ¼ in. slices. Arrange in layers in a pie-dish, sprinkling each layer with cheese, parsley, onion and seasoned flour. Pour in the milk and bake in a moderate oven for one hour. Don't use the oven for one dish only. When the oven is on use it for all your cooking, main dish, vegetables and pudding. You can even fill up the corner by crisping stale bread.

ISSUED BY THE MINISTRY **MF** OF FOOD, LONDON, W.1
P.15

Serve potatoes for breakfast at least three days a week, suggested the UK's Ministry of Food in 1943.

religious grounds. There was a natural passion for growing vegetables during the last two world wars: in the Second World War, home-grown vegetables were said to have saved Britain from a blockade by German submarines – *Tuber über Alles*, mocked one *Punch* cartoonist. The British people were never so healthy, nor their allotments so full, as they were by 1945.

The vegetable garden has a long timeline and as curious a history as any of the world's great gardens. When vegetable plots needed to be measured out, standards were set both by the pyramid-building Egyptians and, in the Middle Ages, by the feet of the first sixteen people to leave the village church. Indeed, if it were not for vegetables, the world as we know it would not exist: both the Spanish and American nations were hothoused on a nutritious diet of maize. Cultivated in Mexico around 2,500 years ago, maize is a relative newcomer to the kitchen garden. Contenders for the prize of being the oldest vegetable in the world include the pea, the lettuce, the leek and the bean, while the award for world's most versatile vegetable must be given to the squash.

In the beginning was the seed. The traffic in vegetable seeds and the methods of marketing them have ranged from setting up a

Country and Western radio station in Shenandoah to the publication of the vegetable gardener's bible, the seed catalogue. Carl Linnaeus and his unfortunate friend Artedi planned to classify not only the world's seeds, but also every living plant and creature. He was as successful as that clever London couple, Mr and Mrs Loudon, who taught the middle classes of the 1800s everything they needed to know about the vegetable.

Vegetable growing comes down to good husbandry, good fences and good, fertile soil. But the kitchen gardener is an anxious soul and inclined to welcome any idea, however eccentric, that might help him or her succeed. The down-to-earth approach works well enough, but over the centuries gardeners have tried some strange methods of raising vegetables, from following the moon's quarters to speaking encouraging words to their plants.

In the new millennium famous vegetable gardens such as Monticello, the home of the American president Thomas Jefferson, in Virginia and Heligan in Cornwall attract increasing crowds of visitors. Home-grown vegetables have become as fashionable as they are fresh: it all serves to demonstrate the welcome return of the private and the public kitchen garden.

According to Rudyard Kipling, the caretaker of these vegetable plots was a patient soul who was to be seen 'grubbing weeds from gravel paths with broken kitchen-knives'. Beatrix Potter and P.G. Wodehouse, who each created their own curmudgeonly kitchen gardener apparently based on real-life Victorian or Edwardian gardeners, suggested the vegetable gardener was a tyrant. But most would agree that the vegetable grower's world is the quiet, contemplative sanctuary that Thomas Jefferson enjoyed. 'I have lived temperately, eating little animal food, and that . . . as a condiment for the vegetables, which constitute my principal diet,' he wrote in 1819.

The kitchen garden is a place to which, like Diocletian, we retire. It is a place of bottom gardens, allotments and potting sheds. It is also a place of quirky and curious revelations. Its tool sheds have been filled with the boys' toys of the garden since at least Queen Victoria's reign, plundered by disgruntled citizens during times of conflict and raided by at least one poisoner who later met his fate on the gallows. But the potting shed, too, has been a place of retreat – and a base from which to wage war on garden pests, especially those celebrated enemies, slugs and snails, which have come in for a range of treatments from the bizarre to the benign.

To make the most of vegetables, they should be eaten as fresh as possible – nothing equals the crispness of home-grown vegetables. However, the trade in 'fruit and veg' is a brisk and lucrative one; the greengrocery or produce aisle is the most profitable one in any supermarket. A business that was once the slow trade of the costermonger has developed into a global market where a garden bean can travel several thousand air miles before it reaches the plate. The key to this expanding market is to pick it quick and keep it cool: the business of preserving vegetables has a strange past – and no more so than when it involved Bob Birdseye's discoveries during his days as a fur-trapper in Labrador. Then, when the year turns and brings each vegetable into season, there are a couple of dozen vegetable events to celebrate.

Emperor Tiberius, John Innes, John Loudon, Rudolph Steiner, Henry Doubleday, Lawrence D. Hills and Popeye: history is full of people with a passion for vegetables. The following stories explore that passion – and the curious history of the vegetable from the medieval monastic garden to the full-on frenzy of Covent Garden in its heyday; from the cathedral-like peace of the walled kitchen garden to the bitter battles of the allotment campaigners; from the muck and magic of the organic gardener to the mysteries of compost.

1

Vegetable Passions

The Political Potato

'I do not hear that it hath been yet assayed whether they [potatoes] may not be propagated in great quantities, for food for swine or other cattle.' So wrote John Worlidge in his *Systema agriculturae* in 1669. 'They are much used in Ireland and America as bread and may be propagated with advantage to poor people.'

Nowadays we all like our potatoes. People in Peru like them too: they have been eating them for 5,000 years. Four-thousand-year-old shards of pottery from the region suggest they worshipped, or at least venerated, the crop as well. The potato, since it became the third largest crop in the world and, after rice and maize, the third greatest source of protein on the globe, is eaten by more people now than ever before.

Yet the fried fish shop was nearly deprived of what Winston Churchill called its good companion – fried, chipped potatoes – by those two other bedfellows, superstition and religious intolerance.

Northern Protestants once declared the potato fit only for pigs and papists, while across the water in Ireland one variety was dubbed the Protestant 'because we boil the devil out'. How on earth did this genial little tuber cause such offence?

Britain in the 1600s was a troubled place of puritanism and superstition. Country women were still being persecuted for witchcraft: Alice Molland from Exeter in the West Country was hanged for witchcraft in 1686. During the Civil War of the 1600s, with royalty and Parliament on opposing sides, families were divided, churches were burned and books destroyed. The works of the devil were all around for those who could see it. The suspicious turned their gaze on the naked little potato with its voluptuous curves and suggestive shapes, not to mention its habit of multiplying and swelling when buried like a corpse in the cold ground. Clearly this too was the work of Beelzebub. The fact that the Bible made no mention of the potato further heightened suspicion especially among Scottish and Irish Protestants.

The Catholic communities, however, were prepared to tolerate the vegetable provided it was ceremoniously planted on Good Friday and liberally sprinkled with Holy Water to keep the devil at bay. By the mid-1700s vegetal battle lines had been drawn between the Catholics who enjoyed their potatoes and the Protestants who preferred their parsnips: during an election campaign at Lewes, Sussex, in 1765 the Protestant candidate openly condemned the Catholic opposition, demanding 'No potatoes. No Popery'.

It did not help the potato's cause that eating them raw often brought on eczema, which was thought to be a form of leprosy. Not surprisingly, one David Davies was predicting in 1795: 'Though the potato is an excellent root, deserving to be brought into general use, yet it seems not likely that the use of it should ever be normal in the country.'

John Evelyn sensibly advocated eating the fruit pickled as a salad, but it was the Revd Gilbert White, one of England's early potato-growers, who recorded a turning point for the vegetable. He noted on 28 March 1758: 'Planted 59 potatoes; not very large roots.' By 1768 he observes: 'Potatoes have prevailed in this little district, by means of premiums, within these twenty years; and are much esteemed here now by the poor, who would scarce have ventured to taste them in the last reign.'

The Germans, after a reluctant start, were won over by the potato after a famine in Prussia. Frederick the Great sent in free potatoes (and armed soldiers to persuade the peasantry to accept them) and the citizens of Offenburg in Germany were so delighted by the arrival of the potato they erected a statue of Sir Francis Drake, holding a potato, in the town square. (It proved too controversial for the Nazis who removed the statue during the Second World War.)

Let them eat potatoes. Parmentier persuaded the French aristocracy to adopt the potato.

But in France the potato suffered a slow start. In the 1700s the peasantry struggled to survive a boom-and-bust economy. In good years they survived. In poor years they starved on a diet of grass roots and ferns. Courtiers who tried to intervene on their behalf gossiped about the callous response of Marie-Antoinette, Louis XVI's queen consort: 'Qu'ils mangent de la brioche' (Let them eat cake). But a pharmacist, Antoine-Auguste Parmentier, had a better idea: 'Qu'ils mangent des pommes de terre. (Let them eat the earth apple or potato). As a former prisoner of war in Prussia, Parmentier had survived on a diet of potatoes and he was determined to introduce it to his motherland. He began by trading on Marie-Antoinette's vanity, persuading her to adorn her hair with a delicate, white potato flower. An alternative version has it that Louis himself wore the potato flower as a buttonhole. Whoever wore the flower, it did the trick – the courtiers fawned in admiration. The gourmets at court were further intrigued when Parmentier arranged a dinner at court where every course included *pommes de terre*.

In 1770 he dealt the Gallic prejudice the final *coup de grâce* when King Louis allowed him to use a field at Versailles to plant a top-secret crop of his precious *pomme de terre*. Guards were posted ostentatiously around the field to protect the crop. The security arrangements doubled people's curiosity and, under cover of darkness, the field was raided again and again. Citizens passed the illicit potato from hand to mouth. The potato had arrived at last and, as if to emphasise the fact, French revolutionaries dug up the Tuileries gardens and planted them with potatoes in 1793, shortly after they had executed Louis XVI with Doctor Guillotine's admirable new invention. Parmentier is remembered still in French dishes such as *Hachis Parmentier*, a meal of minced beef covered with mashed potato.

Back in Britain the potato was receiving a more favourable press. In 1838 William Cobbett observed in *The English Gardener* that the potato 'does very well to qualify the effects of fat meat or to assist in the swallowing of quantities of butter. There appears to be nothing unwholesome about it, and when the sort is good, it is preferred by many people to some other vegetables of the coarser kind.' It was already offering salvation to those in the poor, Celtic west of the British Isles. In Wales the labourer paid his *dyled tato*, a debt of labour to the landowner who permitted him to grow his *tatws* on his land.

When any vegetable becomes central to the economy of a country, it develops its own customs, language and traditions. This was nowhere more so than in Ireland. In the early 1900s Irish families were still sharing their meal of potatoes from the *skib*, the shallow wickerwork bowl that acquired a variety of poetical regional names, including the scuttle (County Clare), the *ciseóg* (County Galway) and the sally saucer (County Louth). The spud, which seems to have acquired its nickname from the broad-pronged fork or 'spud' used to raise the crop, was eaten by Catholics and, eventually, by Protestants alike. Favourites included Epicure, Red Elephant and Champion, 'whilst Arran Banners were fed to the pigs', reports Olive Sharkey in *Common Knowledge* in 1988. But in the late 1700s, the escalating Irish population of eight million souls was putting severe pressure on the subsistence smallholders and their lazybeds of potatoes, planted on the bogland margins. The lazybed was a raised bed, one metre, or three stalks, wide, bordered by a narrow trench. The seed potato was cut in half and planted in March or April with a dibber or dibble. In Cavan and the midlands the dibber was known as a steeveen (from the Irish *stibhín*) and it was the job of the woman of the house who would let it be known that she was out 'guggering' (from *gogaire*, making holes for spuds). Earthing up or *lánú*, where soil from the trench was scooped up and spread across the ridge, was carried out three weeks after sowing and again a month later. The crop was regularly sprayed against blight with a mixture of bluestone and washing soda. Although the cause of blight was not yet understood, the garden author James Shirley Hibberd (who wrote as just Shirley Hibberd) hinted in *Profitable Gardening* at who was to blame: 'Somebody sees it every year; it comes in autumn, it generally comes after wet weather, and *mark*, the most careless growers suffer the most from its attacks. But if some one now lamenting that he has lost half his crop, should rise up and say he bestowed every care upon it, I should say – "You didn't".'

The failure of the Irish potato crop in the 1840s was a national catastrophe and the subsequent famine killed a million and drove another two and a half million on to the emigration ships. Cobh near Cork, the port where the potato had first landed, was, for many

Fifty years after the Famine, disease-resisting potatoes on exhibition in Dublin. (*Suttons Consumer Products Ltd*)

Irish people, their final glimpse of home as the 'coffin ships' bore them off on the twelve-week voyage across the Atlantic.

'When famine and disaster came upon that unhappy country, its citizens took shelter under the Stars and Stripes,' wrote the garden author E.A. Bunyard almost a century later in *The Gardener's Companion.* 'There they fanned the dying embers of hatred against the old country with a result that is with us today. No one . . . will regard a potato as a mere vegetable, but rather as an instrument of destiny.'

The potato had destroyed the heart of a nation; it was soon to transform the look of the countryside. Ireland's regime of inflated rents, unmanageable mortgages and systematic evictions was unsustainable, and, eventually, land reform saw almost three-quarters of the land redistributed among former tenants. While bankrupted owners abandoned their manor houses and walled kitchen gardens, large farm holdings were reorganised so that the fields formed a convenient series of rectangles spreading out behind the farmhouse, the so-called ladder farms, still a familiar sight in Ireland today.

The political potato could cause religious intolerance, save nations from starvation and even alter the lie of the land.

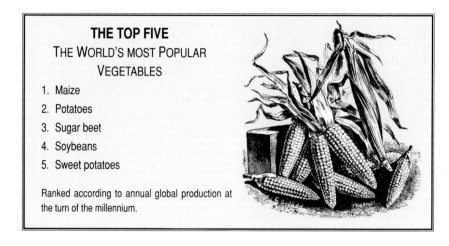

THE TOP FIVE
THE WORLD'S MOST POPULAR
VEGETABLES

1. Maize
2. Potatoes
3. Sugar beet
4. Soybeans
5. Sweet potatoes

Ranked according to annual global production at
the turn of the millennium.

War-Winning Vegetables

Towards the end of the First World War some people in Britain were very, very hungry. Not everyone, however. Those with money to pay the rising food prices ate well enough; those without faced starvation. Rationing the scarce sources of food was the obvious answer, but, with every community in the country mourning its dead, rationing was judged to be politically imprudent. It was finally introduced in 1917, by which time women in Berlin, Germany, were feeding their families on potato peelings.

There were food shortages in the USA too. As the price of a New York onion rose by 700 per cent, housewives took first to the streets to protest, and then to their gardens to dig. Public parks, golf courses and vacant lots fell to hoe and spade in a wave of community gardening. Posters exhorted the nation to 'Sow the Seeds of Victory' and, for the first time, the message went out to the American public: eating greens does you good. America joined the war against Germany on 6 April 1917, as President Woodrow

Wilson told his people: 'Everyone who creates or cultivates a garden helps. This is a time for America to correct her unpardonable fault of wastefulness and extravagance.'

The National War Garden Commission went into top gear declaring on its posters 'Every Garden a Munition Plant', and offering free books on gardening, canning and drying. 'Can Vegetables and Fruit – and Can the Kaiser Too' read another poster. The unrestrained enthusiasm for turning every available piece of greenery into a vegetable plot was not shared by all. The Department of Agriculture regarded the work of the War Gardens agency as amateur interference into what was properly the province of farmers, but, despite its lobbying, 1,500,000 children had enrolled into the United States School Garden Army by the end of the war in 1918.

On the front line in France, meanwhile, the leek had come to the aid of the war effort. The gardens at Versailles were sown with leeks – over twenty-five million in 1917. When the seedlings were large enough for transplanting, they were ferried by military trucks to the Front and replanted close behind the Allied army lines to be grown on and fed to the fighting troops.

War-torn Britain was busy with its own private and public vegetable gardens too. Under DORA, the Defence of the Realm Act, local government requisitioned land to increase the number of allotments from 600,000 to 1.5 million with their campaign Every Man a Gardener. The King, who had hastily changed the family name from Saxe-Coburg-Gotha to the more English Windsor, patriotically ordered the replacing of the decorative geraniums in the flower beds facing Buckingham Palace with potatoes and cabbages. The Church of England gave special dispensation for its congregation to work on Sundays, and the number of vegetable allotments trebled. By the end of the war, the nation was growing a startling two million tons of fresh vegetables. In August 1918 the lawns of London's Kew Gardens yielded nearly 30 tons of potatoes. Three months later on 11 November at 11.00 a.m. the Germans surrendered.

Many an injured soldier returned to nurse his wounds and cultivate his allotment when hostilities ceased. The rest and recuperative value of vegetable gardening was especially important to returning servicemen, trying to overcome the nightmares of their recent experiences.

In the USA by the mid-1920s the backyard kitchen gardening movement was in decline again, partly because of food surpluses and partly because of an Irishman whose family had been driven from his home during the potato famine. This was Henry Ford, the man who popularised the horseless carriage, a machine that, within a decade, saw off the daily deposit of over 1,000 tons of horse manure on the streets of New York. The manure had been enough to enrich every garden in the city.

The European and American economic depression of the 1930s brought the kitchen garden movement back, as British soup kitchens sold penny portions of bread and soup and Americans looked at subsistence gardening to help the poor. Publishers marketed Shilling Guides on frugality and cheap cookery, charitable cookery and cottage cookery, and there was a rush to return to the land, to rely on Mother Nature rather than the factory-owner, who might go bankrupt at any moment.

In town and country during the 1930s, Sunday morning was the traditional time for men folk to tend their allotments and vegetable plots. On 3 September 1939, however, the gardens were silent. Instead the nation was crowded around its wirelesses listening with impatience to a BBC programme on recipe ideas for meals from canned foods. Finally the man they were waiting for, the British prime minister, Neville Chamberlain, came on air.

Britain, he said, had called on Hitler to withdraw his invasion troops from Poland. 'I have to tell you', he said, his speech strained, 'that no

Combined Operations!

Sausage and Vegetables join Forces to make this Delicious Pie

A British nation short of food during the Second World War endured rather than enjoyed its vegetables.

such undertaking has been given and that consequently this country is at war with Germany'. Minutes later air raid sirens sounded out across the capital. It was a false alarm and, for the next seven months, what the French called the *drôle de guerre*, the funny war, began. Nations prepared their weapons and their kitchen gardens.

In America national food surpluses had broken all previous world records. Furthermore nitrogen was more profitably turned into explosives than garden fertiliser and the Agriculture Department campaigned against any move to 'plow up the parks and the lawns to grow vegetables'. Nevertheless, when in 1942 the Burpee Victory Garden Seed Packet went on sale, the seed trade trebled. In 1943, as canned food was rationed, the president ordered the White House

Harvesting the Onion

Everywoman magazine told its readers how to harvest their onions in 1943.

lawn to be dug up and planted with cabbages, carrots, beans and tomatoes. Around four million Americans joined the grow-your-own vegetable brigade.

Having learned its lesson in the First World War, the UK government introduced rationing early on. By January 1940 households had to register at the local shops for their rations of bacon, ham, butter and sugar. Soon all basic foodstuffs were rationed, and the government began a campaign to turn the people into a nation of kitchen gardeners.

'Half a million more allotments properly worked will provide potatoes and vegetables that will feed another million adults and one and a half million children for eight months of the year, so let's get going and let Dig for Victory be the matter for everyone with a garden or allotment,' the Agricultural Minister declared in the stilted language of propaganda. Eleanour Sinclair Rohde, the gardening author largely responsible for promoting the herb garden as we know it today, settled down to write *The Wartime Vegetable Garden*. The Ministry meanwhile circulated cropping plans for a 'ten-rod' allotment, running Dig for Victory exhibitions and setting up demonstration vegetable plots. Every school in the country was encouraged to create its own vegetable patch, and a new, post-war generation of vegetable gardeners was born as these wartime pupils tended their 'tators and peas'.

Vegetables acquired a premium. Home guardsmen in London made hand grenades from potatoes with slivers of razor blades embedded in them. There were recipes for War and Peace pudding (made with flour, breadcrumbs, suet, mixed fruit and a cupful of grated carrot), carrot croquettes, carrot fudge and cake mixtures made with mashed potatoes. There was Potato Pete's recipe book and Woolton Pie, named after a British government minister and made with potatoes, parsnips and herbs. There were mock potato omelettes, mock hamburgers and mock duck, the latter made with mashed potatoes, lentils, beans, sage and onion and shaped like a duck. Vegetable scraps were collected in the street to be fed to pigs raised by neighbourhood groups to supplement their rations. The nation was nervous, hungry, but healthy. 'Most people are better fed than they used to be. There are less fat people,' declared the writer George Orwell at the time. The nation would never be so healthy again.

As the Dig for Victory campaign was launched in October 1939, Sir John Anderson, in charge of air-raid precautions, gave his name to a little corrugated iron shelter that people buried in their gardens – and promptly covered with growing vegetables. The government used its emergency powers to increase the number of allotments to 1.4 million and outlawed the growing of ornamental flowers on them. The green sward covering the moat around the Tower of London was dug up and turned into vegetable plots by the Tower workers.

Vegetable gardening had unexpected risks, especially for those who lived in the south-east, within reach of enemy fighter planes. 'I was out in the garden and I could see this plane coming in. I knew it was a different one to ours from the sound of it. And next thing, there was a line of washing

MINISTRY OF AGRICULTURE

GARDENING "do's" for MAY

★ Do make sure of lots of winter vegetables — especially for the children — by sowing sprouting broccoli, winter cabbage, kale, spinach beet and marrows before the middle of the month.

★ Do sow savoys and early carrots near the *end* of the month.

★ Do sow dwarf beans and dry haricots in rows 2½ ft. apart, allowing 9 inches between plants. Sow also runner beans in double rows 1 ft. apart, 9 inches between plants.

★ Do sow short rows of lettuces and radishes every fortnight ; then you'll always have them fresh for the table.

★ Do put all waste vegetable matter that cannot be fed to livestock, on the compost heap; by autumn it will be valuable manure.

★ Do keep hoeing — to check weeds.

★ Do take precautions against pests.

★ Do post the coupon below for the following *free* 'Dig for Victory' leaflets :

No. 1—CROPPING PLAN
(10-rod plot)
No. 23—CROPPING PLAN
(5-rod plot)
No. 4—PEAS AND BEANS
No. 16—GARDEN PESTS
No. 19—HOW TO SOW SEEDS

The need is " GROWING "—
DIG FOR VICTORY STILL

POST THIS COUPON FOR FREE LEAFLETS

To Ministry of Agriculture (Dept. MC118), Hotel Lindum, St. Annes-on-Sea, Lancs.

Please send me leaflets Nos. ....

NAME.....................

ADDRESS.....................

Dig for Victory. An advertisement in *Weldons Ladies Journal* offers its top kitchen gardening tips in May 1944.

out, about three doors away, and he came down and he peppered all the sheets with the machine gun,' recalled one housewife from Farnham in Surrey. 'They brought him down two miles out of Aldershot and then he was put on view. Sixpence to go and have a look at him,' she adds. It was a contravention of the Geneva Convention on the treatment of prisoners of war, but understandable in the circumstances.

In 1941 the Royal Horticultural Society published *The Vegetable Garden Displayed*. Five years later, it would be translated into German and used to help in the post-war reconstruction of Europe's vegetable gardens. The Americans donated 90 tons of vegetable seed and shipped them over to British allotment holders. In 1942 patriotic gardeners were estimated to be producing a record breaking 1,300,000 tons of fresh food. Did the vegetables win the war? No, but they certainly made people feel better. When canned foods came off the ration list, American war gardeners could afford to relax. Yet vegetable seed sales continued to grow, along with the suburban garden movement. In the early 1950s 39 per cent of American families grew their own vegetables and seventeen million self-confessed gardeners made gardening the nation's most popular hobby. At the same time in the UK around 50 per cent of all gardens contained a vegetable plot.

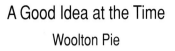

A Good Idea at the Time
Woolton Pie

Lord Woolton was the wartime head of the Ministry of Food and the recipe for Woolton pie was created for the British nation by the then Chef of the Savoy hotel.

Ingredients

1 lb diced potatoes	3 spring onions
1 lb cauliflower	1 teaspoon vegetable extract
1 lb diced carrots	1 tablespoon oatmeal
1 lb diced swede	teaspoon of chopped parsley

Simmer all ingredients together with enough water to cover. When cooked, place in a pie dish, sprinkle with parsley, and cover with potatoes or wholemeal pastry. Bake in a moderate oven. Serve with gravy.

Recipe for a Good Life

Growing vegetables was always considered a useful occupation for the 'lower orders'.

John Claudius Loudon knew a thing or two about the improving effects of the kitchen garden on the serving classes. In a pearls-before-swine kind of declaration he wrote: 'In a state of labour and servitude, man is generally so dull and stupid, that almost every degree of refinement, or sensation beyond that of mere animal feeling, is lost on him. The rich man is happily willing to put his hand in his pocket to help him; but that merely affords a temporary relief from evil.'

The solution was simple, said John Loudon in *An Encyclopaedia of Gardening* (1822). Proprietors should instruct their head gardeners to teach the local cottagers better husbandry. They should 'supply them with proper seed and plants, propagate a few fruit trees' and instruct the cottagers' wives on improved modes of cookery, for example, by 'enlivening the soup with toasted crumbs of bread, a few leaves of chives, and a half leaflet of green celery instead of boiling the ingredients *au naturel*'.

Some seed companies offered cheap and even free seed to the clergy for distribution to cottage tenants. This is from Sutton & Sons' spring seed catalogue of 1863: 'Seeds for distribution to cottagers. These are supplied at a reduction of about one-fourth from the Catalogue prices, with the view of assisting Clergymen and others who desire to encourage their Cottagers in the cultivation of their gardens. For this purpose we send the most useful kinds of Seeds only. Should any of our customers who desire to distribute Seeds among Cottagers not find it convenient to purchase them, we shall be glad to hear from them, in case we have any to spare free of charge.'

Loudon accepted that the labouring classes might need some persuasion: 'It is astonishing how ignorant and how extravagant the humblest classes are in these respects.' However, enforcing improvements with 'adequate motives of hope or fear, of reward or removal' would, he thought, prove a useful incentive and help spread happiness among the poorer households 'at no additional expense to the proprietor'. 'Wretchedness and slovenliness' would soon give way to gardens that were ornamental, neat and above all productive.

One who supported the cause that horticulture improved the body, the mind and the spirit, especially if you were a member of the proletariat, was the Victorian John Ruskin. Ruskin (1819–1900) spanned the Victorian age. He was a writer, critic, painter and gardener. He bought Brantwood in Cumbria in 1871, abandoning its Victorian-style flower beds filled with blooms 'pampered and bloated above their natural size . . . torn from the soil which they loved' and adopting instead a more natural and organic approach. 'What infinite wonderfulness is in the flowers and the trees, considered . . . as the means by which the earth becomes the companion of Man – his friend and his teacher.'

John Ruskin established the Guild of St George to help working people better their conditions and grow their own vegetables. (*Ruskin Foundation: Ruskin Library, University of Lancaster*)

Ruskin was also deeply melancholic – his wife Effy had recently eloped with the painter John Everett Millais, for whom she had been modelling – and deeply philanthropic. One of his lifelong projects was the St George's Company, which, with its stated aim being 'the health, wealth, and long life of the British nation', was concerned that 'the British nation is at present unhealthy, poor, and likely to perish.' Ruskin was convinced that persuading the workers to return to the land and grow their own vegetables was the solution.

The Company, later renamed the Guild of St George, was designed to benefit poor, industrial workers, helping them turn away from the dictatorial factory machines and instead find fulfilment in rustic labours. They would keep the 'hills, streams and fields that God has made for us' as 'lovely, pure, and orderly as we can' and 'gather their carefully cultivated fruit in one season'. Ruskin, who put £14,000 of his own money into the Guild, expected some social improvements among the working classes to attend these good works. It would help, he thought, if the beneficiaries might make 'scrupulous use of sugar-tongs instead of fingers'.

Always underfunded, the Guild nevertheless established rural communities of working people at Totley near Sheffield, Barmouth in Wales and Bewdley in Worcestershire, where seven acres of woodland were given to the Guild by Birmingham merchant George Baker. (Baker would succeed Ruskin as Master of the Guild.)

The land at Totley outside Sheffield was to be worked by a group of socialists who came together after Ruskin had lectured at Ashfield in April 1876. Totley was set up as a Commonwealth under a socialist, William Hamilton Riley. 'St George has now given thirteen acres of English ground for their own,' wrote Ruskin, trusting the families to rely on good work and 'no moving machines by fire', since he had a special loathing for steam engines. But the project failed, and Ruskin had to send his own gardener, David Downs, to turn the operation into a fruit farm instead.

The Barmouth project was more successful. The Guild had been given property by Mrs G.T. Talbot, one of Ruskin's loyal admirers, but the vegetable plots had one drawback. The driving westerly winds, laden with sea spray, played havoc with the buildings – after one visit Ruskin promised to devote the rental income to improving them – and soured the garden soil. One of the tenants, a French exile named Auguste Guyard, came up with a horticultural solution. Guyard was a curious figure. He had been banished from France by the Church, hostile to his plans for creating a new utopian community there. Now, dressed in his grey cloak and wearing a red fez, he would stride around the village frightening small children and dispensing useful advice, including the suggestion that the vegetable gardens be protected with wind breaks 'fenced with furzed hedges'.

Guyard died in 1882 and the following was inscribed upon his tombstone:

> Ci git un Semeur qui
> Sema jusqu'au tombeau
> Le Vrai, le Bien, le Beau
>
> (Here lies a sower who
> Until his death spread the seeds of
> Truth, Goodness, and Beauty.)

Ruskin's Guild died too, but not before Ruskin, in a reaction against the Industrial Revolution and its products displayed so spectacularly at the Great Exhibition of 1851, gave voice to the Arts and Crafts Movement. Its exponents, who included William Morris, Edward Burne-Jones and Dante Gabriel Rossetti, celebrated Ruskin's desire to restore dignity to the craftsperson – and have him cultivate his own kitchen garden.

Allotments for All

In Europe and America the business of growing vegetables in allotments, garden colonies, chalet gardens and worker gardens dates back to the expansion of the cities in the late 1800s and early 1900s. As traditional back gardens were crowded out of town by the encroaching foundries, factories and mills, gardeners were forced to find land away from the home for their vegetables and flowers. In France the poor had to make do with a *lopin de terre*, a vegetable plot squeezed in some urban corner, while the more fortunate found space for the *potager* on the *jardin ouvrier*, grouped together like British allotments on the outskirts of town. The German equivalent was the *Kleingarten*, where rows of vegetables and flowers grew beside the barbecue, the habitable summerhouse and the social club, a model for similar garden colonies that still stretch across Europe from Prague to Paris and Helsinki to Helsingborg.

The word allotment is derived from the Old French meaning to divide out and share, although in the UK its true roots lie in an act of land theft – the enclosures. In the post-medieval days most of Britain was still farmed on an open-field system. By the 1500s, during the reign of Elizabeth I, the process of parcelling-up or enclosing the countryside had begun. Contrary to claims that enclosures were all for the greater good since they produced a more efficient agricultural system, enclosures robbed from the poor and gave to the already rich.

> Inclosure, thou'rt a curse upon the land,
> And tasteless was the wretch who thy existence plann'd . . .

declared the peasant poet, John Clare, as he watched the rural poor grow poorer. Even some of those directly responsible for enclosures, like this secretary to the Agricultural Board, noted with concern that 'the poor are injured, in some, grossly injured'.

Early efforts to compensate the lower classes included the idea of 'allotting' small patches of waste land for the landless labourer to cultivate. In 1806 the nation's first enclosure allotments were provided at Great Somerford in Wiltshire, when 970 acres were enclosed and less than 10 acres provided for allotments. As the legal Acts permitting enclosures were rushed through Parliament between 1760 and 1818, Members of Parliament were petitioned to include allotments in the enclosure Acts. But not until 1819, when

A French gardener harvests produce on his *lopin de terre* squeezed in under the battlements of an old castle.

the number of destitute people threatened to destabilise their communities, were parish wardens legally empowered to rent allotments to villagers. It took another twenty-six years before each Act of Enclosure was required to provide a certain number of 'field gardens' no bigger than a quarter of an acre.

Landowners, meanwhile, had gained more land and a workforce dependent on their largesse. The rural rich were troubled by the notion of allotments. They feared that a labourer with an allotment would steal their seeds. Worse still, the labourer would slyly conserve his working energies during the day, saving them up until he could expend them selfishly on his own allotment. 'The extent of the garden of a laborer ought never to be such as to interfere with his employment as a laborer,' warned Loudon.

Parliament duly insisted that allotments should be small enough to prevent the labourer neglecting 'his usual paid labour'. Still this failed to satisfy many farmers, who threatened to refuse employment to any labourer who kept a parish allotment. Rising crime finally defeated them.

Hitcham in Suffolk was a pretty place, its streets lined with half-timbered farmhouses, its church decorated with a fine fifteenth-century hammerbeam roof. But the rector who preached here in the 1840s, the Revd John Stevens Henslow, was concerned for Hitcham's notoriety – it had one of the highest crime rates in the country. Henslow introduced allotments to reduce local crime. When farmers threatened to blacklist any labourer who would dare rent an allotment, the wise Mr Henslow launched a produce show and invited the great and good among his Victorian parishioners to patronise the show and donate prizes. The annual fruit and vegetable show, always a social leveller, had the necessary healing effect.

The industrialist Titus Salt was another exponent of the allotment. When he built Saltaire on the banks of the River Aire outside Bradford, he gave his mill-workers 800 homes each with a parlour, kitchen, pantry, three bedrooms, an outside lavatory and an allotment 'each not exceeding 15 poles in extent'. John Lawes, who patented the process for manufacturing artificial fertiliser, not only established allotments for the workers on his Rothamsted Estate, but also provided allotment-holders with a club house in which he unsuccessfully tried to persuade the gardeners to drink coffee instead of beer.

The National Agricultural Labourers Union, formed in 1870, actively campaigned for allotments for its members, but, although an Allotment Act was passed by Parliament in 1887, the authorities were still slow to act. The turning point, which saw the workers' frustration boil over into the ballot box, came at a by-election for

Spalding in Lincolnshire in 1887. It had been considered a safe seat for the Conservative candidate until the nomination of an Allotment candidate, Halley Stewart. When Stewart trounced his opponent at the hustings, Parliament promised to find time to consider the vexed problem of allotments. When they prevaricated further, Lincolnshire's local council elections became a battle between allotment supporters and allotment dissenters. The supporters won and Parliament, fearing a rush of allotment MPs arriving at Westminster, pushed through changes. By 1895, at last, the number of allotments had increased by 50 per cent to 482,901. Many were, and still are, set alongside the railway tracks. This was because the second largest suppliers of allotment ground, after the local authorities, were the railway companies, which not only provided allotments for their employees, but let them out to the general public as well.

In the 1900s the allotment movement rose and fell with the economic tides. A National Union of Allotment Holders was founded in 1918 when allotments were still officially classed as being 'for the labouring poor'. In the 1930s, when the Depression saw allotments in strong demand, again, the organisation was amalgamated with the Allotments Organisations Society to become the National Allotments Society. In the 1980s the society had changed its name to the National Society of Allotments and Leisure Gardeners. The change of name reflected a change of style in the allotments: new people with new passions for vegetables were moving in. Immigrant workers from the Asian, West African and Indian communities introduced their own growing skills and vegetables to the allotments. Pat Garfoot and Henry Francis were both Nottingham men with a passion for homegrown vegetables when they took over neighbouring allotments at Hunger Hill. But, while Pat started out growing what his father used to grow, Henry was planting pumpkin,

Two cultures, one passion: Pat Garfoot and Henry Francis on their allotments at Hunger Hill, Nottingham.

beans and calulu (a type of West Indian spinach), just as his parents had in the West Indies. 'Nowadays we have fresh vegetables to go with our regular curry nights up here on the allotments,' said Pat.

Then there are community allotment-holders like Sue Oliver. 'My father was a London butcher and he taught me vegetable gardening on his allotment. You can't beat fresh vegetables, but my husband and I haven't the room to grow our own at home. Now we share our allotment with two other older people as part of a project to promote healthy living.'

And there are still those allotment-holders who hold views little different in outlook from a century ago. Gabriel Jackson runs a small allotment in the West Midlands. 'I grow vegetables because it's part of that hunter-gatherer thing – I want to supply my family with good, fresh vegetables. Out of season vegetables in the supermarket make me angry: it takes away the pleasure of growing your own. My father grew his vegetables, his father probably did and I hope one day my son, Sam, will too. Growing veg makes you feel good.'

Community allotment-holder Sue Oliver tending her plot in the rural West Midlands.

Vegetable Radicals

Growing vegetables as a form of protest has a long and respectable past. When a clothier, Gerard Winstanley, was ruined during the Civil War in England, he was reduced to herding cattle for a living. In 1649, outraged by the poverty he saw around him, he and his community of 'Diggers' invaded common land in 1649 and proceeded to dig it up and plant vegetables.

In Cobham on the little heath the digging still goes on
And all our friends, they live in love, as if they were but one,

he rhymed.

Oliver Cromwell's Lord Fairfax sent in the army to deal with this vegetable riot and destroy the diggers' parsnips, carrots and beans. Another nine colonies suffered the same fate. Winstanley appealed to Cromwell, the Lord Protector: 'If the wasteland of England were manured by her children, it would become in a few years the richest, the strongest and the most flourishing country in the world,' he predicted. If the poor were well fed they would soon be 'making discoveries to benefit all'; the nation could even enjoy a free state medical service, suggested Winstanley. His pleas were ignored along with his insight into a national health service, and, with the restoration of the monarchy, Winstanley slipped from view and died in obscurity.

Three centuries on and a new group of diggers went into action. These were supporters of Friends of the Earth who in the 1970s organised demonstration 'dig-ins' on empty ground to highlight the fact that good land was lying idle while waiting lists for allotments were lengthening. There were still 121,000 people on the allotment waiting lists in 1980 when other demonstrations began, this time against the siting of American Cruise missiles in the UK. While women set up protest peace camps at Greenham Common, the husband of one protester, Chris Mattingly, loaded his Massey Ferguson tractor and plough on to the back of a trailer and set off for RAF Mildenhall, a major US air base in Suffolk. Under the nose of the guards he unloaded his tractor, hitched up the plough and turned over a symbolic acre of land at the base. He returned later and sowed a crop of wheat, which, in late summer, was harvested, threshed and presented to one of the aid agencies for export to a famine-struck region in the developing world, Bangladesh.

During the 1900s the pace and scale of scientific advance could be measured against the fact that, while the first manned flight had taken place in North Carolina in 1903, regular space travel was a reality by 2003. And yet, throughout that century hundreds of thousands of people continued to die of starvation because they could not grow enough vegetables. Concerned by the plight of the poor and the impact of agribusiness and genetic modification on global seed stocks, a Frenchman Dominique Guillet began saving old varieties of vegetable seed in 1994.

After a spell making products for the Bach Flower Remedy company, founded in Wales in 1930, he started growing old vegetable varieties on an estate in the Auvergne. His company, Terre de Semences, was dedicated to *la libération de la semence et de l'humus* (the liberation of seeds and humus), but he was forced to shut down the company (and establish a seed library instead) when the French Ministry of Agriculture demanded a registration fee for each of Terre de Semences's

The early vegetable protestors, Gerard Winstanley and his Diggers, took property law into their own hands.

2,000 seeds. This was despite a European Union directive on promoting the production of traditional vegetable varieties and the fact that, in the previous century, the West had lost 98 per cent of its traditional vegetables. 'Let us not speak of transgenic plants:

one page would not suffice to express our anger. To find and ask the true questions we would need a whole book and we have not got the time or space. We have far too much to do on the land so as to produce honest seeds so that growers can regain their freedom and their choice,' wrote Guillet.

Terre de Semences was followed in 1999 by Association Kokopelli, an organisation devoted to saving old varieties and distributing seed, free if possible, to the developing world. Within its first two years Kokopelli had distributed 150,000 seed packets in Asia, Africa and South America.

The Biggest Is Best?

Allotment-holders from Hunger Hill in Nottingham once raised roses alongside their vegetables to help pay the rent. And even before they organised Britain's first national rose show at the General Cathcart Hill Inn in 1860, the produce show was gaining in popularity. John Lawes instituted a produce show for his allotment-holders at Rothamsted, just as the Victorian clergyman the Revd Henslow introduced his annual fruit and vegetable show at Hitcham in East Anglia to repair social divisions within the community. Grand international shows attended by royalty were at the top of the social calendar, with village shows, attended by the lord and his labourer, at the bottom. But in every fruit and vegetable show size was all.

The Shrewsbury Show was one of literature's more famous horticultural events and the scene of Lord Emsworth's pumpkin triumph in P.G. Wodehouse's *The Custody of the Pumpkin*. While Emsworth, or rather his gardener, Mr McAllister, finally took the prize from his neighbour, Sir Gregory Parsloe-Parsloe, former head gardener Keith Ruck revealed how, in real life, the prize winning

First prize. The produce from Sutton & Sons seed collection won the day at the Reading Horticultural Show of 1897. (*Suttons Consumer Products Ltd*)

was not always above board. 'There was a lot of cheating going on. Like if you got wireworm in a carrot, you take some soap and an old carrot, mush him up to get the right blend of colour and then use that to cure the blemish. Course when I was judging I used to look out for things like that because I knew how it was done.'

Ruck's father regularly took gold medals in the Cottagers' Class at Shrewsbury during the 1920s. 'A lot of parsnips were grown in barrels, in holes barred down through the soil and filled with leafmould and sand so the parsnips didn't have to fight against anything. During the shows then, the parsnips would be rested in the old bungalow baths, or zinc baths, laid on damp sacking. The parsnips were the full length of the bath and some of the tapering ends would be hanging over the end.'

On show. A prize display at Holland's Floriade gardens.

But the showman's garden, he remembers, was not an orderly place. 'We never had a tidy garden. You got leeks growing in pipes, kidney beans growing in wire cages so they would grow nice and straight, and we were always digging into the rows so you never had anything perfect to look at.'

The growing of prize onions had a particularly deleterious effect on the appearance and the scent of the garden: 'The show onions were started in the winter, in seed. Growing onions was a sore point with my mother because one of Dad's friends was a butcher from Abergavenny who done his own slaughtering. We used to have drums of blood and soak the ground with it 'til it go near a green or a black colour. It didn't used to smell very sweet either. The show onions would be hoed before Dad went to work and again when he come home, his chief aim being to get the air to them. Then we would water with his homemade fertiliser, sheep daggin' water. He took hundreds of prizes.'

Another prize-winning grower was Bernard Lavery of Llanharry in Wales, who once held nineteen world records and ten British records for growing giant vegetables. He grew a cabbage that weighed 56.24 kilograms, a marrow of 49.04 kilograms, a 12.73-kilogram radish; a 9.10-kilogram cucumber, an 8.25-kilogram Brussels sprout and, in 1996, a carrot that weighed 5.20 kilograms. He had grown a pumpkin that weighed 322.06 kilograms, while the world record, as judged by the World Pumpkin Confederation, was 514 kilo-grams, until Howard Dill of Nova Scotia in Canada grew a 600-kilogram squash from a strain of the Atlantic Giant variety. The world's longest tomato plant also eluded him. A tomato plant, grown hydroponically at Lancashire in May 2000, measured 19.8 metres or 65 feet.

Artists and their Kitchen Gardens

Garden historians often look on artists as a potentially inspiring group of gardeners. Being creative individuals, artists are expected to bring the same visual and conceptual gifts to their gardens as they do to their art. Those expectations were fully realised in the case of Claude Monet (1840–1926), whose Normandy garden Giverny has become one of the world's most famous. Monet shared his horticultural enthusiasms with another painter Gustave Caillebotte. When Monet and Caillebotte proposed visiting a friend, the friend wrote back: 'I'm glad you are bringing Caillebotte. We'll talk about gardening since Art and Literature are nonsense. Earth is the only thing that matters.'

The earth, especially that which lay beneath his *potager*, mattered greatly to Monet. He was a *bon viveur* who, like many French

Giverny, Monet's flower-filled garden in Normandy. The artist maintained his own vegetable garden nearby.

patriarchs, demanded fresh vegetables at the table. When he was wealthy enough, he bought another house at Giverny in the neighbouring Rue de Chêne, simply for its walled kitchen garden. It was also equipped with forcing frames, a cellar for storage and mushroom growing and a fertile soil for his turnips, tomatoes, peppers and beans.

Monet was a prodigious painter who worked from dawn to dusk, but he would take time out every day to visit his vegetable garden on the Rue de Chêne and select the produce that was to be picked first thing the following day and served at his supper table.

His Impressionist colleague Pierre-Auguste Renoir, meanwhile, was overseeing the planting of his own kitchen garden in Provence.

In 1906 an ancient olive grove on a smallholding, Les Collettes near Cagnes-sur-Mer, was due to be cut down and replaced by a market garden. Prompted by the threat to the old trees, Renoir bought Les Collettes. (According to his son, the film-maker Jean Renoir, the painter was a born conservationist who would take care not to tread on even the humble dandelion when out for a walk.) The painter created a studio within the garden, and, while he worked, Aline, his former model and lover and now the mother of his three children, laboured in their kitchen garden. She manured the soil with grape skin and dung from her goat, rabbits and hens and paid special attention to their permanent artichoke beds. And when the time came she always made sure the first pressing from the old olives at Les Collettes was ceremoniously presented to her husband.

Monet and Renoir were self-made men. Renoir had worked as a poor apprentice in a Parisian porcelain factory when he was 13, while Monet had laboured hard and long before his paintings began to sell for serious money. Their mutual friend Gustave Caillebotte, however, had been born with the proverbial silver spoon in his mouth. His fame as a painter waned in proportion to his consuming passion for gardening and, when his family estate was sold, Caillebotte bought an estate at Petit Gennevilliers on the banks of the Seine, north-west of Paris, turning his Impressionist garden into a vast horticultural experiment. Aside from nurturing rare orchids, he experimented with planting arrangements, both in the flower borders and the walled kitchen garden, putting to the test the theories of Michel-Eugène Chevreul: Chevreul's critical analysis of colour and his notions about complementary colours had profoundly influenced the Impressionist painters and would later influence the work of the painter turned garden designer, Gertrude Jekyll.

Monet's and Renoir's gardens have survived, but of Caillebotte's there is nothing except a corner of the old family estate at Yerre, now a municipal park, and a section of the walled kitchen garden recreated from Caillebotte's own paintings and planted with neat rows of vegetables interspersed with dramatic strips of marigolds.

While the French Impressionists were enjoying the fruits of their vegetable patch, an English poet and an American president were sharing a passion for growing peas. The poet was William Wordsworth – his sister Dorothy frequently noted in her diary that her brother was out staking his peas. The US president was Thomas Jefferson, a keen gardener who liked to compete with his neighbours to grow the first crop of peas fit for the plate. By staggering his planting and growing at least fifteen different varieties of English peas, Jefferson could enjoy fresh peas from mid-May to mid-July. But a Mr George Divers usually grew the first crop and had the privilege of throwing a celebration dinner. Jefferson finally beat Mr Divers, but, in a masterful show of modesty, he kept the news to himself and dined with his supposedly victorious neighbour as usual. 'It will be more agreeable to our friend to think he never fails,' Jefferson told his family.

Arcimboldo's Royal Portraits

Some of the strangest representations of the vegetable in art are to be seen in the paintings of Giuseppe Arcimboldo. Little is known about Arcimboldo. He was born in Milan in 1527 and at 38 became a painter at the royal courts of the Hapsburgs. The artist, judging from his representational self-portraits, was a good-looking fellow, but he pursued a peculiar obsession with vegetables when he turned to the portraiture of others, in particular those of his last patron, Rudolph II. Arcimboldo had already trialled these curious vegetable portraits under the patronage of Maximilian II in 1569. In his final commission in 1591, two years before his death, Arcimboldo painted an allegorical portrait of Rudolph where the monarch's face was composed entirely of vegetables and fruits. His patron is said to have been delighted by the images.

2

Origins and Losses

A Vegetable Timeline

People have grown vegetables for 8,000 years at least. One theory – and it remains only a theory – supposes that vegetable cultivation was precipitated by the first famine, triggered by a world population too large to continue feeding itself on hunting and gathering alone. The natural balance between communities and wilderness had been reached and passed. From then on, the human race would have to grow their own food if they were to survive. Once they had settled and begun to harvest the wild fruits of the neighbourhood, people started to cultivate plants in a sustainable fashion.

If we contrive to represent the last twelve millennia as twelve months of a calendar year, we would find the Natufian people, who lived in the Middle East to the west of the River Euphrates, already gathering their wild cereals in January of that fictitious year. At the other end of the timeline, around 27 December, the United Kingdom would be mourning the death of a keen vegetable grower, Gertrude Jekyll. She died in 1932.

In our mid-January or 10,000 BCE the ice sheets that had locked down Europe and North America finally began to melt. In the March of our vegetable year the earliest recorded vegetables were growing around Palestine. The early civilisations had settled in the Middle East, building their palaces and pyramids, towns, ports and, of course, kitchen gardens close to the irrigating rivers of the Tigris, Euphrates and Nile.

By mid-April, vegetables were being grown around the borders of modern Iran and Iraq. In Crete the kitchen garden was established by May, in China and Mexico by June, and the Indus Valley of eastern India by August, 2500 BCE in real time.

By mid-July (3500 BCE) agriculture and its sister horticulture had been carried across the Indus plain by the Indus Valley civilisation. We know more about the visible surface of the moon than we do of

Vegetables were being harvested in Turkey at least 4,500 years ago.

this mysterious culture. Archaeologists have uncovered some of its village factories, but scholars are still wrestling with its language and deliberating on whether it should be read from the left or the right. The scholars have established that by 1700 BCE (or early September) the civilisation had collapsed, perhaps because of political instability, a shift in the course of the great Indus river itself, some other natural disaster such as an earthquake, or a combination of all three.

By mid-September (1500 BCE) the ancient Egyptians, planting flowers in their vegetable plots, were growing gardens for pleasure as well as purpose. A literary Greek garden 'full of fruits, also sweet figs and bounteous olives' appears in early October in Homer's *Odyssey*. Later that month, or around 300 BCE, according to paleobotanists, there were celery, beet, carrot, brassicas and asparagus being grown in the southern Mediterranean and peas, vetch, wheat and barley in northern Europe.

The Romans acquired their gardening crafts from the Greeks and by the end of October (100 BCE) the Latin vegetable garden was as highly productive as it was highly advanced. As the empire expanded through Europe they introduced their own favourites, including garlic, onion, leeks, lettuce, mustard, parsnip, skirret (a sweet-tasting edible root), turnip and radish. The collapse of the Roman Empire apparently led to the collapse of the kitchen garden. This may be more due to a lack of documentary evidence than a paucity of vegetable-growers, but we must wait until mid-November and the rise of the monastic garden before finding Britons enjoying a decent plate of vegetables again. They were still not described as vegetables – in early medieval times a herb described any garden plant useful as a pesticide, a medicine or for the pot. Not until the third week in November (around the year 700) does the word 'vegetable' creep into common use.

Culinary historians are still looking at establishing the genetic continuity between modern and medieval vegetables, but we would recognise many of the edible plants grown in the kitchen garden twelve centuries ago. Skirrets, garlic, plain-leaved parsley and the medieval broad bean, which can be traced back to the horse bean, were all on the menu. The medieval garden burgeoned with self-seeding salad crops such as fat hen and dandelion, the latter still a common enough salad crop. 'My mother used to cover the young dandelion with a dish to blanch them and keep the dogs from peeing on them,' recalls one young woman from Malvern, while a French woman from Cholet remembers: 'Grandmother harvested *pissenlit* and served them with a salad dressing. They made you piss.'

Yellow or red onions, sown as seed or planted as sets, were grown along with green onions – that is, any small or bull-necked onion eaten fresh rather than lifted and stored. They came under an assortment of names, including ascalonia, fissiles, scallion, chibol, clumping winter onions and holeke. Holeke was the ever-ready onion, *Allium cepa var. perufile*, occasionally confused with the Welsh onion, which was not Welsh at all, but 'foreign' from the Old German word *Welsch* meaning foreign. The true ciboule or spring onion, *Allium fistulosum*, was a later arrival to Europe from Asia in the 1700s, or mid-December of our vegetable year.

By early December the Renaissance kitchen garden in Europe was well advanced. Meanwhile the last of Spain's Moorish leaders, Boabdil, had surrendered the keys to the city of Granada to his Christian conquerors. He left with a tear on his cheek, by the pass known as Ultimo Suspiro del Moro, the Moor's Last Sigh, after the legendary remark of his mother: 'You do well to weep like a woman for what you failed to defend like a man.' Boabdil left behind a rich horticultural inheritance, still to be seen in places such as Valencia, where the *huertas verduras*, the irrigated lands, grow hectare upon hectare of vegetables under the gaze of derelict Moorish castles.

By mid-December, when Drake claimed California for England, the two-way vegetable traffic between America and Europe had reached fever pitch. For the next ten days, until Christmas Eve, the kitchen gardens of both nations flourished. In 1850 – or shortly after our Christmas Day – the Irish bogland potato crop failed.

Post-Christmas and, apart from a growing frenzy in the kitchen garden during two world wars, the home-grown produce of the kitchen garden steadily diminished under a tidal wave of convenience and processed food. Vesta introduced the first convenience meal, a chicken curry, to the UK housewife in 1962. But by the very end of December or the late 1900s, north Europeans had rediscovered what Mediterranean Europe had known all along: the best tasting vegetables are the ones you grow yourself.

Out of the East

Today upwards of seventy different vegetables can be grown in the kitchen garden and, until the opening up of the Americas in the

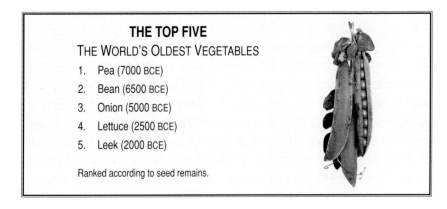

THE TOP FIVE
THE WORLD'S OLDEST VEGETABLES

1. Pea (7000 BCE)
2. Bean (6500 BCE)
3. Onion (5000 BCE)
4. Lettuce (2500 BCE)
5. Leek (2000 BCE)

Ranked according to seed remains.

sixteenth century, most originated in the Middle East. The story of how they reached the vegetable plot is a long and sometimes confusing one. Take the **globe artichoke** and its apparent sister, the **Jerusalem artichoke**. As for the globe artichoke, *Cynara scolymus*, that looks like what it is – an edible thistle. It first came into the kitchen 4,000 years ago when it was cultivated in the Middle East, in the fertile crescent that lay between the Nile and the Indus.

To the Greeks it was *kardos* or *skolumos*, to the Romans *carduus*, which explains why the Italians still enjoy their *cariofi*. One Roman painter

Artichokes, once ranked as the top vegetable aphrodisiac, growing in the fields around Valencia, Spain.

depicted Priapus on a fresco weighing his monumental member on a set of scales against a globe artichoke, presumably a reference to the artichoke's ancient reputation as an aphrodisiac. The English name originates with the Arabian name *al-kharshuf*.

The Jerusalem artichoke, *Helianthus tuberosus*, however, was related neither to Jerusalem nor the globe artichoke. A member of the sunflower family, the Jerusalem artichoke came from what was to be Europe's second richest source of vegetables, the Americas. The edible part of the *kaishcucpenauk*, as the Algonquin Indians called it, is the tuber and it was Samuel de Champlain, one-time governor of French Canada, who reported that the *kaishcucpenauk* tasted of artichoke. The confusion was compounded when the appellation Jerusalem was added, as a corruption either of the Italian for sunflower, *girasole*, or of Terneusen, the Dutch village between Antwerp and Ostend that dispatched artichokes to England in the early 1600s. By 1617 it was reported to be grown by one John Goodyer in Hampshire. The *kaishcucpenauk* originated on the Great Plains of North America, where it was cultivated by native Americans, and by the time European settlers arrived it was growing wild from Georgia to Canada. The Pilgrim fathers, however, viewed the Jerusalem artichoke with as much suspicion as the twentieth-century allotment-holders who referred to it as the 'fartichoke' for its flatulent reputation. John Gerard had no time for the plant either: 'In my judgement, which way soever they be drest or eaten, they are meat more fit for swine, than men.' In fact the Jerusalem artichoke is very nutritious and a safe vegetable for diabetics.

Returning to the Middle East, **Asparagus**, *Asparagus officinalis*, was another plant brought in from the wilds by the assiduous gardeners of that fertile region

Asparagus was first cultivated in the fertile region around the Nile and the Indus, while Sutton's Perfection was said to be 'common in the restaurants of Paris' in the 1890s. (*Suttons Consumer Products Ltd*)

around the Nile and the Indus. Two thousand years later its priapic appearance had earned it its lustful, tumescent Greek name *asparagos*. It was introduced to Europe by the Romans. (Pliny reportedly bought three giant asparagus heads that weighed around half a kilogram.) The diarist Samuel Pepys, who died in 1703, reported buying 'a bundle of sparrow-grass' in London's Fenchurch Street for one shilling and sixpence, and growers and market traders alike still sometimes refer to it as grass. It was always regarded as a vegetable extravagance: '*The asparaginous class of esculents* may be considered as comparatively one of luxury,' wrote Loudon in the 1800s. 'It occupies a large proportion of the gentleman's garden, often an eighth part; but does not enter into that of the cottager.' He recommended the grower devote 'five square poles of ground, planted with 1600 plants' for a yield of 'six to eight score heads daily'.

Some kitchen gardeners find it difficult to grow, but the wild *Asparagus officinalis* proved to be a determined coloniser, making a stand just about anywhere from Morocco to Manchester. As economically important to Venetian traders as their home-blown glass (farmers around Bassano were busy with their asparagus beds in the 1500s), asparagus was taken to the Americas by the early settlers. It made little impact on the American diet, however, until it was canned and turned into a cheap, but poor, substitute for fresh asparagus.

Other vegetables raised in the Nile and Indus region included the beetroot, carrot, celery, pea and turnip. The **beetroot**, *Beta vulgaris*, was growing here 4,000 years ago. While the Greeks ate the leaf of the beet, the Romans enjoyed its swollen red root, which explains why the English ate their 'Roman

Sutton's Blood Red beetroot.

47

beet' in Tudor times. In 1597 John Gerard wrote of the 'great red Beete or Romaine Beete': 'the beautiful roote which is to be preferred before the leaves, as well in beautie as in goodnesse.' Given a good feed, he claimed, beetroot could grow to 3.5 metres (12 feet). By 1656 the beetroot, now being grown by the gardener and plant hunter John Tradescant the younger, was referred to as the '*beet rave* or beet-radish' from the French *betterave*.

A direct relative of the beetroot, the **mangle**, mangold or mangle-wurzle, still grown as a prize exhibit at agricultural shows in the UK, started life in the German Rhineland as a chance hybrid between the beetroot and a white-stemmed chard. The great gnarled roots were fed to cattle, but not before they had been lifted and weathered in a clamp long enough for their natural toxins to have leached away.

The **carrot**, *Daucus carota*, was a younger vegetable than the beetroot, but only by 1,000 years or so. Unlike the potato, it was welcomed into the British kitchen garden of the 1500s: 'Sowe Carrets in your Gardens, and humbly praise God for them, as for a singular and great blessing.' So instructed Richard Gardiner in his 1599 *Profitable Instructions for the Manuring, Sowing and Planting of*

Sutton's Early Gem carrot.

Kitchen Gardens (manuring meant cultivating). Three and a half centuries later the propaganda character of Dr Carrot was making a contribution to the British war effort. When Britain was plunged into darkness by the night time blackout in an effort to hide from enemy bombers, the carrot, packed with vitamins that benefited the optical nerves, was a natural aid for those fumbling their way home in the dark.

The red carrot, however, was just one of a rainbow selection of coloured carrots that ranged from scarlet and purple to white and yellow. The Romans referred to them as both *daucus* and *carota* (which is why Linnaeus accorded them both names), and, while their conquering legions almost certainly brought them through Europe, the European tribes of Saxons, Celts, Angles and Vikings seem to have ignored the beneficial carrot for 1,000 years. It was left to the Moors to reintroduce the purple carrot from the Middle East in the 900s. The Spanish Moors were growing carrots by the 1100s, the Germans and Dutch by the 1300s, the English by the 1400s and the American Virginians in the 1600s, when colonists first sowed the seed there – and let loose the wild carrot, which spread across the continent. The Americans and the Chinese would eventually become the world's major carrot-growers, but it was industrious Dutch gardeners who, in 1720, produced the Long Orange Dutch cultivar, the prototype for our modern varieties.

It was Moorish gardeners too who were responsible for developing **celeriac** (*Apium graveolens var. rapaceum*), the swollen-rooted vegetable that became such a popular plant in central and eastern Europe and carried the now forgotten alternative name of Dutch or Hamburg parsley. But true **celery**, *Apium graveolens*, was yet another vegetable that emerged from the Indus plains 4,000 years ago. By Roman times there was talk of the little pot herb called *apium* being used to flavour fish, as a garnish in sauces and as a decorative head gear for their champion games players. But it was left to the future generations of Italians to develop their *sedano*, the crisp, thick stalked celery that we eat today. It may have been introduced to northern Europe by an Italian, Giacomo Castelvetro, who, living in exile in England in 1614, described how to grow and prepare it. When it reached America with the early settlers it too

Sutton's Prince of Peas.

bolted into the wild and spread far and wide.

The **pea**, *Pisum sativum*, was another vegetable that originated in the Middle East. Four thousand years later the Greeks were enjoying their *pisoi*. Subsequently the Romans introduced their *pisum* to the rest of Europe. Early peas had coloured flowers and small pods and were grown as a field crop, but gradually the white flowered garden varieties were developed with larger peas. Thomas Hill (who also wrote under the curious pseudonym of Didymus Mountain) in his *Gardener's Labyrinth* of 1577 proposed successional sowings of 'Rounseval pease' in spring, the name derived from the large seeded peas named after Roncesvaux Abbey in France.

Dried peas ground into flour and mixed with wheat or rye were traditionally used to make bread. They would be soaked overnight and turned into pease porridge or pease pudding. In Scotland pea flour, known as peasemeal, would be mixed with water and milk, or whey, and baked on a griddle to make bannocks. The habit of eating the under-ripe peas arose, not in the freezer packs of the 1900s, but in the 1600s, during a craze at the court of Louis XIV, who had a passion for *petits pois*.

Although the pea had been brought into cultivation and improved in the Middle East, it was one of the earliest domesticated plants. Bronze Age families, for example, were eating peas 5,000 years ago. Could it lay claim to be one of the world's first garden vegetables? Three other vegetables cultivated in what was the fertile Middle East could also be considered as odds-on favourites: the lettuce, the onion and the leek.

In the 1800s an Edinburgh doctor was marketing his *Lactucarium*, an 'opium juice' made from **lettuce**: the name of the lettuce, *Lactuca* *sativa*, recalls the fact that the Romans too used it as a mild narcotic. Their lettuce exuded a bitter sap or latex that, having properties similar to laudanum, promised a good night's sleep – the name came from the Roman *lactuca* or milk.

The lettuce, a relative of the chicory family, was brought into cultivation far earlier than Roman times. Cos or 'Roman' lettuces were pictured on 5,000-year-old Egyptian tomb reliefs (although they earned the term Roman or their French name *laitue romaine* when they were brought to Avignon by the papal courts of the 1300s). Theories abound as to why the English should have named the 'cos' lettuce after the Greek island of Kos, but, since Kos was the birthplace of the physician Hippocrates, it may have been to mark the medicinal qualities of the vegetable. An Italian recipe from 1614 recommended quartering the lettuce, dressing the quarters with oil, salt and pepper and then roasting them over a charcoal grill before eating them sprinkled with orange juice. By the 1800s lettuce was being harvested all year round. Even now, with butterheads, crispheads and cut-and-come again varieties, there are as many different lettuces as there are months in the year.

Another contender for the oldest garden vegetable is the **onion**. To 'know your onions' is to know all. The Indian Brahmin knew the onion well enough to avoid it, and anything else 'arising from impurity', altogether. The onion, *Allium cepa*, is a member of the lily family; it probably originated in the central Asia regions, although no one knows for sure. Spread by traders throughout the world, it

Sutton's White Heart cos lettuce.

was part of the staple diet in Greek and Roman times, the latter, possibly, giving it the name *unio* for singularity.

The **leek**, *Allium porrum*, like the onion a member of the lily family, may be one of the world's most ancient vegetables, but it is certainly one of the main ingredients in the world's oldest recipe. A 4,000-year-old inscribed Babylonian tablet suggests using crushed leeks to spice up a lamb stew. The Greeks called the leek *prasa*, the Arabs *kurrats* and the Romans, who brought them into northern Europe, *porrum*. Why the Celtic Welsh, who successfully held out against the invading Romans, should have adopted the leek as their national emblem is something of a national mystery, but, given their love of song and oration, it may have been associated with the leek's throat-soothing, mucilaginous qualities: the Roman Nero, derided as a *porrophagus* or leek-eater, ate leeks to improve his voice. Since he also invented the art of sycophantic applause, his success may be thrown into question.

Out of India

Two important vegetables, the aubergine and the cucumber, came into cultivation from the Indian subcontinent. The Indian **aubergine**, *Solanum melongena*, is a member of the Solanum family along with deadly nightshade, *Atropa belladonna*. The aubergine was not welcomed when first it arrived in England, partly because of its fearsome family connections and partly because it was blamed for a succession of ailments from piles, halitosis and liver obstructions to a poor complexion and, ultimately, leprosy. But, suggested John Parkinson in the 1600s, it was perfectly safe if boiled first in vinegar.

In Sanskrit it was *vatin-gana*, a wind-killer, but it was also known as a melongene, Jew's apple, mad apple, brinjal and egg plant (early varieties were small, white, egg-like fruit rather than the deep purple of modern varieties). Its Hindustani name was *bungan*, which became the Arabic *al-badingan*. When the Muslims swept through Egypt and North Africa in the 700s and replanted the local vineyards with their own vegetables, they brought it into Spain (the Spanish still call it *berenjena*), Sicily and the Languedoc region of France.

The **cucumber**, *Cucumis sativus*, came out of the foothills of the eastern Himalayas. This runs counter to the claim of William Tyndale, who, when he translated the Bible in the 1500s (he was strangled and burned as a heretic for his efforts), asserted in the Book of Isaiah that the daughter of Zion lodged 'in a garden of cucumbers'. In the twenty-first century the vegetable is infamously featured on some of the more salacious web sites, but, grown in England as early as the fourteenth century, the cucumber was regarded as an enemy of lust by the sixteenth-century garden author Thomas Hill. He also claimed that a thunderstorm would cause the cucumber to bend. The cucumber was so-called after

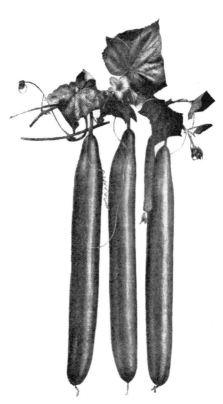

The cucumber, an 'enemy of lust', was brought to Europe from the foothills of the Himalayas. (*Suttons Consumer Products Ltd*)

the Old French *cocombre*. However, the 'little wild cucumber' of the West Indies, although related to the cucumber, and better known as the **gherkin**, *Cucumis anguria*, was carried from south-west Africa to the West Indies in the 1600s with the slave trade. It earned its name from the Dutch *augurkje*.

The Roman Emperor Tiberius had a particular passion for the *cucumis* and the Romans created fantastically shaped cucumbers by encasing the young fruits in wood, wicker or clay casts. There was to be none of this nonsense in the Victorian kitchen, where the cook insisted upon long, straight fruit, achieved by hanging lantern-like glass cylinders around the growing cucumber.

Out of Rome

When the conquering Romans arrived on the shores of Britain in the year 43 CE, they introduced not only their civic buildings, their villas and their roads, but also their ornamental gardens and their favourite vegetables. For example, the wild **cabbage**, *Brassica oleracea*, has uncertain origins, although the Greeks, Romans,

Sutton's Earliest garden cabbage.

Moors and Italians were primarily responsible for its spread and it was the Romans who brought it to northern Europe along with radishes, parsnips, turnips and carrots. (After the fall of the Roman Empire the root crops were largely forgotten and it was left to the wholesome cabbage and onions to fill a hungry gap of a thousand years until the

Renaissance.) A polymorphic plant is one that, chameleon-like, can take on different forms. The cabbage is a polymorphic triumph and there are six main cultivars: non-heading kales, heading cabbages, swollen stemmed kohlrabi, Brussels sprouts, broccoli and cauliflower. But leave them growing together for long enough and all six will cross-pollinate and gradually revert to their wild cabbage cousin.

Each of the brassicas seems to have developed as a regional favourite. **Brussels sprouts**, for example, were first recorded in Belgium around 1750, hence the name. 'At Brussels they are sometimes served at table with a sauce composed of vinegar, butter, and nutmeg, poured upon them hot after they have been boiled,' reported an incredulous Loudon. In north-eastern Europe, *choucroute* or *sauerkraut*, made from finely shredded cabbage leaves pickled with juniper berries and sea salt for three weeks in stone crocks, became a favourite. The **cauliflower** was brought into Spain in the 1400s by the Moors and was growing in London a century later. The **broccolis** were always an Italian favourite. Phillip Miller described it as Italian asparagus in 1724 and it was Italian immigrants who took their beloved broccoli to America.

Kohlrabi, possibly the vegetable described as a 'Corinthian turnip' by Pliny the Elder, was promoted as a novelty vegetable in Victorian times. Jane Grigson in *The Vegetable Book* of 1978 took a less-said-the-better approach to kohlrabi: 'There are better vegetables than kohlrabi. And worse.' Which may explain why much of the kohlrabi grown in Britain was fed to cattle.

The old English name for the **turnip**, *wort*, belies its ancestry as a member of the brassica family. In Ireland the Gaelic *neip* was an important crop, sown in drills, which ran the length of the field, alongside the potato ridges. The seed, sown and weeded by hand, would be dipped in highly toxic red lead to protect it against birds.

Even in Northern Europe the sheltered Roman villa garden was a hothouse when it came to vegetable growing.

The Romans also enjoyed their *pastinaca* or **parsnip**. The Frenchman still enjoys *la panais*, the German his *pastinake*, the Russian his *pasternak* and the Italian his *pastinaca*, since it was the Romans who introduced the parsnip, *Pastinaca sativa*, to these countries. The English linked the French *pasnaie* with the turnip or neep, and John Gerard gave it his qualified support: 'the Parsneps nourish more than do the Turneps or the Carrots, and the nourishment is somewhat thicker; but not faultie nor bad.' The parsnip sweetened in the ground, its starch being converted to sugar by frost action. It was eaten on Ash Wednesday, cooked to accompany salt cod. Thomas Hill in his *Gardener's Labyrinth* recommended sowing 'parsnep' in well-manured ground in high summer for eating in Lent the following year. Used to make wine and to sweeten cakes in the days when honey was the only major source of sugar, its high sugar and starch content has ensured it has been grown in the kitchen garden ever since.

Curiously, when the parsnip reached Virginia in 1609, it was held in high esteem by the native Americans but largely ignored by the north Americans. Perhaps this was because the native Americans in the south-west and Mexico were accustomed to making a meal out of the baked, ground root of the wild parsnip. In Britain meanwhile, and so long as north European Protestants still regarded the potato as the inferior food of the Roman Catholics, the parsnip was the preferred accompaniment to roast beef.

Another seasonal accompaniment were **broad beans**, *Vicia faba*, which, like the faba, field, winter, tick or horse bean, had been cultivated since biblical times. Ancient broad-beanlike seeds 8,500 years old have been found in the Middle East, and the seeds probably reached northern Europe in the hand luggage of the Roman centurion. Originally a black bean, the broad bean was a valuable crop, since the seed could be eaten fresh or dried and the plant's nitrogen-fixing qualities endeared it to the gardener. It was such a prize crop that, by the Middle Ages, the crime of stealing beans from open fields carried the death penalty. The bean had its own revenge, for it had a fierce reputation for flatulence: 'Broad beans are very nutritious, but are not easily digested and should not be given to invalids,' warned the cautious author of one kitchen encyclopaedia. The poet William Butler Yeats was untroubled by its notoriety:

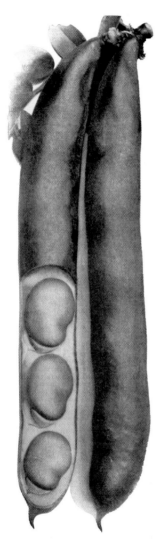

Brought to Britain by the conquering Roman, the broad bean has retained a place in the vegetable bed ever since – despite a fierce reputation for flatulence. (*Suttons Consumer Products Ltd*)

I will arise and go now, and go
   to Innisfree,
And a small cabin build there,
   of clay and wattles made;
Nine bean rows will I have
   there, a hive for the honey
   bee,
And live alone in the bee-loud
   glade . . .

he wrote in 'The Lake Isle of Innisfree', published in 1893.

Exercising poetic licence, Yeats did not mention whether he preferred the broad bean or one of the many garden beans that had originated on the other side of the world – America.

Out of America

European gardeners owe a debt of gratitude to the American Indians for their protein rich maize, squash, potatoes and **beans**. The new American civilisation owes its very existence to them.

Forty years before Yeats penned his poem, that contemplative gardener Henry David Thoreau was planning his own Indian bean patch, on the shores of Walden Pond at Concord, Massachusetts. 'What shall I learn of beans or beans of me? I cherish them, I hoe them, early and late I have an eye to them and this is my day's work.'

Thoreau, however, did not eat his beans, but sold them to buy rice. He was growing 'the common small white bush bean', one of more than fifty varieties of *Phaseolus*, all originating from the Americas and embracing French, navy, *flageolet*, snap, *haricot vert*, scarlet or runner bean (*Phaseolus coccineus*), and the Lima or butter bean (*Phaseolus lunatus*).

The Webbs' Spring catalogue for 1888 noted: 'The Kidney Bean, *Phaseolus vulgaris*, has been cultivated for a considerable time, but there is uncertainty as to whether it was known in Europe before the discovery of America, where the genus is strongly represented.' It was not. The kidney bean, which still grows wild in South America, came into Europe in the sixteenth century stashed alongside the Spanish *conquistadores'* captured gold. When the scarlet flowered runner bean reached the royal gardens of England during the reign of Charles I it was grown purely for its pretty flowers. It was not until the early 1700s that Philip Miller, who ran the Chelsea Physic in London, advocated cooking and eating the green pods.

Spanish *conquistadores* also brought the **capsicum pepper**, *Capsicum frutescens*, to their mother country in the 1500s. They called it the *pimento*, and the Italians took the *pepperone* to heart, making it an indispensable ingredient in their kitchen recipes. The capsicum, when dried and crushed, was popular elsewhere in Europe because it served as an acceptable substitute for pepper at a time when true black peppercorns were proving too expensive for the kitchen table.

When Columbus brought back yet another 'new' Latin American crop, **maize**, the old Mexican name, *cintli*, was substituted for the

Spanish *maiz* instead. (Columbus had discovered the crop growing in Cuba, where it was known by the local Indians as *maisi*.)

Zea mays, a member of the grass family, was to become one of the world's most popular crops. Variously known as corn, sweet corn, Indian corn, mealies, corn on the cob and popcorn, it was originally cultivated by native American Indians and sustained not only the Toltecs, Aztecs, Mayas and Incas, but also the 'new' American civilisation: in 1810 the population of America was around six million. Largely fed on maize, it had risen to ninety-four million a century later.

Within a century of reaching Spain, maize had spread across the globe. William Cobbett spoke of it growing in Britain by 1803, and, although it was, and still is, fed to cows, it became, in the form of cornflakes or corn on the cob, a favourite British food. Maize also generated its own legendary figures. There was the Mexican goddess of plenty, Cinteutl, and the American Indian Mondamin, a green giant who was killed and buried by Hiawatha. The maize plant that rose up from Mondamin's grave saved Hiawatha's people from a winter's starvation. Because the sugar in the corn starts to convert

Maize has traditionally attracted its mythical figures, including the contemporary Green Giant, first used to promote corn over a century ago. (*Green Giant, The Pillsbury Company*)

to starch the moment it is picked, sweet corn is best when picked and eaten fresh from the kitchen garden: 'the principle of the lathe is adopted in eating them,' explained Edward Bunyard helpfully in the 1930s.

Bunyard was also an enthusiastic supporter of another American import, the marrow. 'We may use it for jam, pies, soup, etc., its merit being its placid acceptance of all flavours.' **Marrows, pumpkins** and **squashes** are all members of the cucurbita genus, which originated in the Americas and had arrived in Europe within fifty years of Columbus' voyages. Seeds have been found on ancient Mexican sites and the cucurbits formed a staple part of the diet, along with maize and beans, of native American Indians all along the east coast of America. When the first Pilgrim Fathers landed at Cape Cod, Massachusetts, in 1620, those who survived starvation were rescued by Patuxet Indians, who taught them how to grow pumpkins among their corn, burying a herring beneath the crop as fertiliser. In October 1621 the settlers ate a ceremonial meal of boiled pumpkins as a thanksgiving for their survival. Although the recipe has been improved, the custom has continued.

The name squash came from the Algonquin Indians and the pumpkin from the Greek, and later Old French, *poumpon*. In terms of alternative uses, the cucurbita are the world's most versatile vegetables: in their different forms, they have served as cups, bottles, the back-scrubbing loofah, soaps, household ornaments, yak fodder and even the legendary birthplace of the Burmese people.

While we are used to a pale- or yellow-fleshed **potato**, *Solanum tuberosum*, those growing still in the wilds of South America, from where they originated, range in colour from yellow and red through to purple and black. The horticultural Incas built terraces and aqueducts to feed their potatoes, which were cultivated as a storage crop and which complemented the maize, grown at lower levels. (Growing potatoes for seed in a cold, blight-free climate benefited the tubers and explains why Scotland traditionally produced the best seed potatoes in Britain.)

The Spanish explorer Gonzalo Jiménez de Quesada is claimed to be one of the first Europeans to have encountered the fertile spud around 1536. The Spanish discovered the truffle-like tubers, or *turmas de tierra* as they called them, in the tropical forests of Columbia's northern Andes. From here the potato was almost certainly carried back to Spain and up the River Guadalquivir to Seville in 1573. (There is some confusion here, as the sweet potato, *Ipomaea batatas*, which had been discovered in Haiti by the explorer Columbus, was also being imported to southern Spain around this time.) The potato travelled on to Italy as *tartufflo*, and into France as *cantoufle* or *truffe*, but it arrived in England in the 1590s by a different route and with a different name.

John Gerard mentions the 'potatoe of Virginia' in 1597. Gerard, a London barber-surgeon, was an enthusiastic gardener who not only managed several of London's society gardens, but also looked after his own plot of ground in Holborn. Here he grew 'all the rare simples' and 'strange trees, herbes, rootes, plants, flowers, and other such rare things'. When in 1596 he catalogued his plants, the year before his famous *Herbal* was published, the potato appeared in the inventory. When the second issue of the *Herbal* was published, Gerard dedicated it to Sir Walter Raleigh, who, some say, introduced the first pinch of tobacco and the first potato to Britain.

'To England the potatoe found its way . . . being brought from Virginia by the colonists sent out by Sir Walter Raleigh in 1584, and who returned in July 1586, and "probably", according to Sir Joseph Banks, "brought with them the potatoe",' explained John Claudius Loudon in 1824.

The story goes that Raleigh came by both potato and tobacco through another English knight, Sir Francis Drake. Drake, who had been battling with the Spaniards in the Caribbean, sailed for

England after collecting some provisions including potatoes at Cartagena, Columbia. Drake also picked up a group of Virginian colonists who had had enough of the hard life and wanted to return home. Drake's ship, *The Golden Hind*, berthed in Cork in southern Ireland, leaving a few of his potatoes with Raleigh, who grew them on at his Youghal home in County Cork. Raleigh's gardener is said to have sent the poisonous potato fruit rather than the root to the kitchen. The rest arrived in Britain, possibly in Lancashire, but Gerard, confusing the returning colonists with the vegetable, cultivated them under the name *Battata Virginiana*, the Virginian potato.

The **tomato**, *Lycopersicum esculentum*, like the potato, came from South America. The ancient ancestors of the fat, red tomato grew wild on the riverbanks of Peru and Ecuador and grows there still. When it spread into Central America and Mexico, resourceful American Indians brought it into cultivation. Spanish *conquistadores* came across what the Indians called *tomatl* and shipped the fruit back to Seville, from where it travelled to Italy. In 1544 one Italian writer recommended cooking the tomato 'like an eggplant – fried in oil with salt and pepper'. He called the fruit *mala aurea* or golden apple. Linnaeus classified it as *L. esculentum*, but its supposed links with mandrake (*Mandragon autumnalis*), a notorious narcotic that reportedly shrieked when pulled from the ground, branded the tomato a dangerous fruit, good only for table decoration. 'In Spaine and those hot regions they used to eat prepared and boil'd with pepper, salt and oil; but they yield very little nourishment to the body and the same naught and corrupt,' explained John Gerard. John Parkinson described it in terms with which those prejudiced against the tomato would agree: it was, he wrote, 'full of slimie juice and waterie pulp'.

In Europe the tomato became what the French called *pomme d'amour* or love apple, a reference to its supposed aphrodisiac

It took an American court case to decide that tomatoes were 'in the common language of the people . . . vegetables'.

qualities. Its powers to promote promiscuity earned it yet another name – mad or rage apple. Although the American president Thomas Jefferson was content to grow them in his Monticello garden in the 1780s, the tomato clearly needed further promotion. In 1820 Robert Gibbon Johnson helped it along by publicly eating a basket of tomatoes on the steps of the courthouse in Salem, New Jersey, to dispel the myth that the tomato was poisonous. The argument over whether it was a fruit or a vegetable (and thus earns a place in this book) was settled by an American court of law. John Nix, seeking to avoid a 10 per cent tax on vegetables imported to the USA, claimed the tomato was a fruit. The Supreme Court in 1893 ruled that, while the tomato, like the cucumber and squash, was a 'fruit of a vine', these were all 'in the common language of the people . . . vegetables which are grown in the kitchen garden'.

Out in the Cold

One vegetable that was almost lost to the kitchen garden is the **skirret** (*Sium Sisarum*), a perennial tap-rooted plant that originated in China and was grown in Britain for over four centuries. In Scotland the skirret was cultivated under the name of 'crummock'. The gentleman gardener John Worlidge described skirrets as 'the sweetest, whitest, and most pleasant of roots' in 1682. These fleshy roots had been cultivated for centuries and Shakespeare makes mentions of them in his *Merry Wives of Windsor*. Although still eaten in China and Japan, the root had already disappeared from one English kitchen garden calendar of 1876.

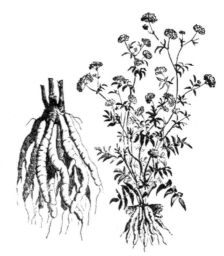

Eaten and enjoyed for over four centuries, the fleshy-rooted skirret had been dropped from the seed catalogues by the 1880s.

The **swede**, on the other hand, slipped into the culinary wilderness in the mid-1900s as the result of cheap school dinners and a heavy reliance on the vegetable during the Second World War. Jane Grigson, in her *Vegetable Book*, judged 'the watery orange slush . . . unredeemable by drainage or butter'. In the root bed the swede is a close cousin of the turnip and was commonly confused with it in the vegetable taxonomy. When the swede was taken to America, it arrived with its Swedish name of ram's root or *rotbagga*. The turnip, from the Latin *napus*, became in the 1500s the *neip* in Britain, but when, on Burn's Night, a haggis was put on the hob along with *neips*, the *neips* were swedes and not turnips.

What's in a Name?

The curious names of some vegetables shed light on their histories: perhaps when returning Crusaders brought seeds of the

Persian *ispanai* or *isfanai* home, it was mispronounced as our spinach. But did the French bean really originate in France? Did the eating of cucumbers cause such offence that someone had to invent a burpless variety? Why do Americans grow zucchini and the British courgettes?

The bean provides a starting point for some linguistic origins, and confusions, of vegetables. Take the dwarf kidney bean, also known as the French bean and in France *haricot vert*, a tender bean eaten pod and all, and *haricot jaune*, podded and harvested for the seed. *Haricot* comes from its Aztec name, *ayacotl*, but it became the French bean because it was the Gallic gardeners who cultivated it. The French *flageolet* bean was so-called either because it looked like a flute or *flageolet* or was a corruption of *Phaseolus*. (It was the French, too, who gave the 'Hasty' pea, a large and early variety, its name – from *hâtif* or early.)

Phaseolus, the Latin name for a small, fast-sailing craft, referred to the canoe-like shape of the bean pod, while the kidney bean itself earned its name from its similarity to that part of the body.

The climbing bean was known to gardeners at the court of Charles I as the 'runner' bean. It had been collected in Virginia, USA, by the King's gardener, John Tradescant, and given to the monarch as a decorative plant. In its homeland, however, it became a string bean, a reference to the stringy seams that run down each side of the pod.

When the *Phaseolus* began to supplement the old-fashioned field, Celtic and broad bean (all varieties of *Vicia faba*), John Gerard spoke with surprise of being able to eat them 'cods and all'. Favourite varieties in the early 1800s included the Windsor, so-called by Huguenot gardeners simply because Windsor happened to be a profitable place to grow them, and the Mazagan. 'Sow the first crop of early [pea] varieties, rolling the seed in red lead, and filling the drills half full over the peas with chopped furze [bracken] or chopped barley

The enthusiastic sixteenth-century London gardener John Gerard found great pleasure in eating the new American beans 'cods and all'. (*The Royal Horticultural Society*)

chaff. Sow dwarf Peas in pot. Plant Mazagan Bean, and treat in the same way,' advised the *Illustrated Guide for Amateur Gardeners* of 1876.

Mazagan was a small Portuguese settlement on the coast of Morocco and seed from the settlement promised to produce a well-flavoured, early crop. The English naturalist the Revd Gilbert White was already well ahead of the pack when he wrote in his *Garden Kalendar* on 2 November 1754: 'Started ten rows of Mazagan-beans (never planted in England) in the field garden.'

As for the potato, another vegetable championed by the good vicar of Selbourne in Hampshire, it was the Peruvians who referred to it as *papas* and hence its one-time French name, *la papas des Péruviens*. In Wales the potato became *pytatws* and in the Scottish vernacular *tatties*, which sounds more like the Spanish name for the sweet potato, *batatas*.

Another linguistic throwback concerns the 'ridge' cucumber, so-called for its habit of climbing over the old-fashioned ridges in the ridge-and-channel system of vegetable growing. The cucumber, especially in the raw, was viewed with some suspicion by English Victorian gentlemen, who preferred to eat it stewed and served in a white sauce. The arrival of a burpless variety calmed all fears of an accidental, tea-time belch and the uncooked cucumber went on to become the staple sandwich filling at vicarage tea parties.

And finally, why do Americans, whose 'squash' seeds were taken to Europe in the 1500s, now find themselves eating 'zucchini'? It was the Italian immigrants who reintroduced the courgette to its place of origin, along with their name for it.

The Secret of Selling Seeds

The seed is the beginning of all things.

'*Germination* is that act of operation of the vegetative principle by which the embryo is extricated from its envelopes, and converted

A Good Idea at the Time
Container Growing

The popularity of container gardening has grown in proportion to the diminishing size of the average garden. But in Roman times, the men and women who looked after the Roman Emperor Tiberius' gardens turned container gardening into craft. The emperor was mad about cucumbers and expected, as emperors do, to be able to eat them at any, and every, time of the year. Terrified of the emperor's wrath, his gardeners invented a system of growing the cucumbers on portable beds. If cold weather threatened, the beds were wheeled inside to safety. On cool days they were taken out of doors, and sheltered behind windows made of mica, a translucent stone cut into sheets for the purpose.

into a plant. This is universally the first part of the process of vegetation. For it may be regarded as an indubitable fact, that all plants spring originally from seed.' So wrote John Claudius Loudon in his *Encyclopaedia of Gardening*. It was published in 1822 shortly after the seed merchants, Messrs Sutton & Sons, had distributed a printed list of the seeds they sold. It was not the nation's first seed catalogue – seed-sellers and nursery people had been advertising their wares in newspapers and magazines for a half a century or more – but it was the first to offer kitchen gardeners a current price list and useful advice on when and how to plant their vegetable seed. It was also the first of many devices designed to ensure that a well-thumbed copy of the seed catalogue survived the growing season and was still on hand in winter when it was time to reorder seeds.

At first seed companies relied on the fine and often inspirational line drawings of their artists and the enthusiastic sincerity of their copywriters to sell their wares. 'With great satisfaction we now introduce a new White Kidney which we have had under trial for several years. It was raised by the late Mr Clark, the raiser of our Magnum Bonum, Abundance, and other heavy cropping varieties, and combines the high quality of Victoria in its best days with the productiveness of White Elephant. The yield has astonished experienced growers to whom we sent small parcels for trial.'

The subject of this entry in a Sutton's seed catalogue was the potato, Sutton Perfection. Sutton's and other catalogue editors were quick to learn the value of publishing testimonials alongside advertisements for 'The Student Parsnep', the 'Red-top Mousetail Turnip' and the 'Prince of Wales, a heavy cropping Pea, which has long been popular with amateurs and cottagers.' 'I have cut Cucumbers from your Berks Champion three weeks earlier than any of my neighbours,' boasted the Revd J.R. Barlow of Pertenhall, Kimbolton, with a singular lack of modesty in a Sutton & Sons catalogue for 1881.

The people who paid the seed bills were the gentry, even if it was their head gardeners who ordered them, and the catalogues could be both obsequious – 'Gentlemen are respectfully invited to have price from us before ordering elsewhere' – and charitable: 'From your beautiful and valuable Amateur's Guide, I have made a common labouring lad into a most excellent practical Gardener,' wrote Mrs Parsons from The Castle, Buttevant, County Cork. 'I do not see anywhere nicer work or so good things as he grows, and all his education has been from one of your Guides.'

Colour printing processes transformed the appearance – but not the prose – of the seed catalogues in the second half of the 1800s, just as the American seed market, previously a profitable source of income for European seed-growers, developed its own seed industry. In their battles for supremacy, the 800 or so US seed merchants proved to be innovative marketeers. There were free gifts of seeds and more testimonials: 'The package of Vandergaw Cabbage you sent me did much better than the Large Late Flat Dutch.' There were promotions, price wars and prizes: 'We offer, for 1888, CASH PRIZES of $25.00 and $10.00 for the two largest onions raised from seed

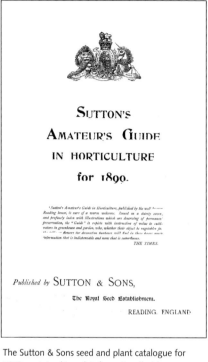

SUTTON'S

AMATEUR'S GUIDE

IN HORTICULTURE

for 1890.

' Suttons's Amateur's Guide in Horticulture, published by the well known Reading house, is sure of a warm welcome. Issued in a dainty cover, and profusely laden with illustrations which are deserving of permanent preservation, the "Guide" is replete with instruction of value to cultivators in greenhouse and garden, who, whether their object be vegetables for the table, or flowers for decorative purposes, will find in these pages much information that is indispensable and none that is superfluous.

THE TIMES.

Published by SUTTON & SONS,

The Royal Seed Establishment.

READING. ENGLAND.

The Sutton & Sons seed and plant catalogue for 1899 contained 'much information that is indispensable and none that is superfluous', declared the *London Times*. (*Suttons Consumer Products Ltd*)

purchased of us this year – the onions, or reliable affidavits of their weights, to be sent to us before Nov. 1st,' promised the authors of the Burpee catalogue, which in 1888 ran to 128 pages, most of them devoted to vegetables.

Then there were slick slogans. 'Seeds That Yield are Sold by Field' was the catch phrase of Henry Field, who had started out on horseback selling seed around Shenandoah in the 1890s. By the 1920s he was running his own country music radio station and selling his seeds on air.

In France meanwhile, one of the nation's most senior seed firms, Vilmorin, devised a clever strategy for selling its products: the picture. The company was based on an old family firm, Le Febvre, run by Pierre Geoffroy. In 1782 Geoffroy's daughter Claude, or Mâitresse Grainière (the Seed Mistress) as she was known, and her husband Pierre Andrieux, botanist to Louis XIV, opened a shop on the Mégisserie Quay in Paris. The business, later run by their daughter and her husband, Philippe-Victoire De Vilmorin, became Vilmorin-Andrieux and later Vilmorin Co. Responsible for introducing the field beetroot and 'rutabaga' or swede to France, Philippe-Victoire was also a good publicist. He not only commissioned watercolours to illustrate their catalogues and seed packets, but also ordered a collection of artificial vegetables to be exhibited at the Paris Universal Exhibition in 1855. Made of plaster, each was a perfect replica in weight and colour of the vegetable itself.

Seed sales people learned to be economical with the truth, picturing on their seed packets and catalogues magnificently exaggerated versions of their produce. The underlying aim was, as it has become and ever more will be, to appeal to the aspirational gardener.

It was not always so. Plain vegetable seed was being sold, without any trimmings, from The Strand in London in the late 1600s. The garden historian John Harvey has traced at least five nurseries in and around the capital at that time, the largest, London and Wise, occupying 100 acres of what would later become the site of the Albert Hall and the South Kensington Museum.

The sale of vegetable seed, measured by the bushel and hundredweight, was a lucrative business worth over half a million pounds a year. While it was concentrated on the south-east, each region contributed its own regional specialities to what Loudon called the Middlesex seed market 'held twice a week in a large roofed space in Mark-lane. The purchasers are the London retailers, or the wholesale dealers for their country customers.' Kent gardeners brought their radish, kidney beans, turnips, 'toker or Sandwich beans' and onions; Berkshire men brought their cabbages and white-skinned or Reading onion seeds, while in Worcestershire and Warwickshire the market gardeners took their seeds of white onions, asparagus, cucumber and carrot to the Birmingham markets. In Leicestershire, Loudon noted, 'the farmers, tho often rich, have seldom good gardens'.

Seed was also sold by stallholders, costermongers and barrow boys at country markets across the land. Those who chose not to buy, or could not afford to do so, carefully collected and stored their own seed in mouse-proof drawers and rat-proof safes, despite the advice of garden writers such as Shirley Hibberd: 'the professional seed-grower will beat you nine times out of ten. . . . and if you deal with none but respectable seedsmen, and avoid the cheap rubbish that is vended in odd corners, you will save a good deal of labour.'

Thomas Tusser, however, was in favour of trading seed locally:

> One seed for another to make an exchange
> With fellowly neighbours seemeth not strange,

he suggested in 1580.

Home seed was selected, not from some stunted individual, which had been missed during the harvest, but from the earliest, healthiest and most vigorous vegetables. Carrots and cabbages, which formed seed in their second year, were lifted whole in their first autumn. The carrots, after their foliage was cut back, were buried or clamped in beds of peat or sand. The brassicas, their root balls still intact, were tenderly wrapped in cloth and hung from the rafters of a dry shed, where they held their breath until spring. Then they could be replanted and their seed harvested when it was set. Alternatively, the cabbage could be buried outside. 'Market gardeners and many private individuals, raise seed for their own use,' wrote Loudon. 'Some of the handsomest cabbages . . . are dug up in autumn, and sunk in the ground to the head; early next summer a flower-stem appears, which is followed by an abundance of seed. It is mentioned in Bastien, that the seed-growers of Aubervilliers have learned by experience, that seed gathered from the middle flower-stem produces plants which will be fit for use a fortnight earlier.'

Well ripened and dried, the seed would keep for six to eight years, he added, confirming the conviction that seed improved with age. For example, three to four years was judged ideal for cucumber seed, while soaking the seed in sheep's milk or mead (the alcoholic drink made from fermented honey) prevented the fruit from turning bitter.

Success was guaranteed if seed was 'sown dry and set wet' and poor soil was usually blamed for the failure of seed to set true or perform like its parent. Once Carl Linnaeus revealed that cross-pollination between different varieties of the same species was the problem, seeds people began to exploit this characteristic to improve or enoble vegetable seeds.

Webbs' Seeds announced the arrival of their new, cross-breed pea, the Wordsley Wonder in 1888.

This wonderful Pea is the result of crosses between Advancer, Little Gem, and Prizetaker, and whilst possessing all the good qualities of the two former varieties, it has both the constitution and productiveness of the latter. As a first early Pea for large gardens, it is unequalled, and its convenient height and cropping properties render it indispensable to the amateur.

So the practice of improving seed, although not necessarily for the good of the gardener, continued until, in the 1960s, the F1

Sutton & Sons offered vegetable and flower seeds 'specially packed for the colonies'. (*Suttons Consumer Products Ltd*)

hybrids that had been developed in the 1920s began to emerge. The F of F1 stood for *filia*, Latin for daughter, and the seeds promised to revolutionise the kitchen garden, developed as they were by crossing two selected lines to produce vigorous growth from dependable seed. But, like the genetically modified seed that would follow in its wake, it had one great advantage to the seed merchant and one disadvantage to the gardener: it did not set true seed. The gardener was obliged to return to the seed catalogue year after year.

And it is the gardener's little winter bible, the seed catalogue, that reveals how times have changed in the seed industry. When Vilmorin-Andrieux published its 100-page catalogue of vegetables suitable for 'cold and temperate climates' in 1885, the list included 58 beets, 145 cabbages, 74 onions and no less than 170 different peas. A century later in 2003 a British seed catalogue could offer only 6 beetroot, 20 cabbages, 5 onions and 10 varieties of peas.

Carl Linnaeus and the Classification of Vegetables

Jan: 20. Hot-bed works very well. Hard frost for two or three days: now ground covered with snow. One of the hyacinths in the glasses seems to promise to blow soon.

22. On this day, which was very bright, the sun shone very warm on the Hot-bed from a quarter before nine to three quarters after two. Very hard frost.

29. On this day the mercury in the weather-glasses, which had been mounting leisurely for many days, was got one full degree above settled fair in the parlour, & within half a degree of the same in the study.

The Revd Gilbert White's *Garden Kalendar* for 1758 reflects the winter preoccupation of every vegetable gardener: the cold. In 1758 gardeners across the northern world watched the mercury fall at night and rise by day. Then, as now, they measured the temperature against the celsius scale devised by Anders Celsius. For reasons best known to himself, however, Anders calibrated his scale so that nought represented the boiling point of water and 100 degrees its freezing point. Today we would be complaining of a mild frost of 103 degrees had it not been for a chance meeting between Anders's uncle, the genial Olaf Rudbeck, and an impoverished Swedish student, Carl Linnaeus, at Uppsala in 1729. Rudbeck took the 22-year-old in and fed him. It was Linnaeus who persuaded Olaf's nephew Anders to reverse his calibration.

Linnaeus not only set the standard calibration for the kitchen garden thermometer; he also learned how to grow bananas successfully in the Netherlands and set the standards for modern botanical gardens such as Kew and the Eden Project in Cornwall. But his most important contribution to the vegetable world was to devise a system of classifying vegetables and every other living form.

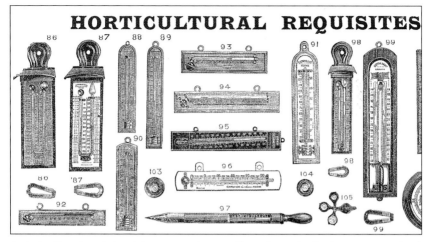

A nineteenth-century choice of thermometers for vegetable gardeners. But for the intercession of Carl Linnaeus, Celsius would have recorded a frost as 100 degrees. (*Suttons Consumer Products Ltd*)

While one colleague described his work as 'lewd and licentious', Linnaeus had the satisfaction of having his system of classification adopted around the globe. We use it still today.

Carl Linnaeus was born in a simple turf-roofed timber cabin at Råshult near the shores of Lake Mökeln in the southern province of Sweden on 23 May 1707, the oldest child of Nils Ingemarsson Linnaeus. Nils had adopted the name Linnaeus when he attended the university at Uppsala, taking the title from a favourite tree that had grown at a former family home. The tree was a lime or linden; forty years later it would become *Tilia cordata*, thanks to Linnaeus.

Nils was the parish priest and a fanciful gardener. He once created a curious raised bed to represent the family dining table with shrubs to portray the dinner guests sitting down to a meal. Carl was as intrigued by this horticultural oddity as he was by the natural world in general. Even at 5, out walking with his father, Carl would quiz Nils on the local names of plants. Nils is said to have reprimanded the boy and told him to commit the correct names to memory.

He also gave the child a plot of his own to cultivate. The garden is a good educator and Carl, like his younger brother Samuel, became a committed naturalist and gardener. This passion for gardening had unfortunate consequences for Samuel Linnaeus. Some years later when Carl failed to follow in his father's footsteps and become a priest, his tutor told his parents that the young man's academic shortcomings were entirely due to his horticultural obsession. Fearing that Samuel would prove a second disappointment, Linnaeus's mother banned Samuel from meddling with plants. (The boy turned his attention to bees instead, a subject on which he would become a world authority.)

Carl went to study medicine rather than theology at his father's old university in Uppsala. Here he became friends with Peter Artedi, a fellow student who shared his fascination for the natural world. The two young men hatched an ambitious plan: together they would classify all God's plants and creatures in a systematic fashion. Until then every vegetable and plant had had a variety of local or vernacular names and several, sometimes conflicting, Latin names. A Greek physician, Dioscorides, had diligently named some 500 plants in his *De materia medica* around the time of Christ, but it took almost 1,000 years before his work was disseminated through first the Arabic and then the Latin world.

Linnaeus and Artedi divided the task of classifying the animal and plant kingdoms between them and swore that whoever finished first would then come to the aid of his friend. But in 1735 Artedi died when he fell into an Amsterdam canal and drowned. Linnaeus took on all the work himself. By the time he died in 1778 (some say of overwork) Linnaeus had introduced a system for naming vegetables – and every other plant – that endures to this day.

Botanists and naturalists were agreed that plants fell into families. Onions, leeks, and garlic, for example, belonged to the allium family; beans and peas to the legume family; cabbages and cauliflowers to the brassica family; sweetcorn to the grass family. What Linnaeus did was to introduce a two-word name for every plant within the families.

Plant families could be subdivided into distinct groups (or genera) and Linnaeus used the genus for the first name: *Pastinaca* from the Latin *pascare* (to feed) for the parsnip, for example, and *Pisum* for the pea. Each group or genus could be divided again, this time into species. Linnaeus used his second Latin name to denote the species, so the garden pea became *Pisum sativa* as distinct from the Mediterranean pea, *Pisum elatium*. Finally, each species could be further divided to include cultivated varieties or cultivars. As well as inventing a standard use of Latin words for every plant, Linnaeus also provided an international starting point for the old botanical names when he published his *Species plantarum* in 1753.

Linnaeus classified the genus and species of plants according to the number of stamens and stigmas, a 'sexual system' of classification. One of his friends was John Siegesbeck, a St Petersburg academic after whom Linnaeus named the Sigesbeckia. But the two fell out after Siegesbeck denounced his former friend's work as 'lewd'. How, he ranted, could onions be up to such vegetative immorality? What was worse: how could young people be taught 'so licentious a method' of classification? Despite the 'loathsome harlotry' of his system, it was adopted universally and Linnaeus became a household name.

Linnaeus also showed the kitchen gardener that the successful cultivation of any vegetable depended on duplicating as closely as possible the plant's natural origins, soil and climate. (He would later advise the curators of botanical gardens to keep separate hot, warm and cold glasshouses as well as an outdoor area so that they might

Carl Linnaeus invented a 'lewd' system for classifying vegetables and all other living forms. But his methods finally won the world over. (*Royal Horticultural Society*)

replicate local growing conditions, which laid the foundations for contemporary dome gardens such as the Eden Project.)

In spite of his celebrity status, Linnaeus was a modest man. For his funeral arrangements he stipulated: 'Entertain nobody at my funeral, and accept no condolences.' But when he died on 22 January 1778, his instructions were ignored. A stately funeral was held at Uppsala Cathedral and even the King of Sweden came to pay his respects to the man who had given a name to every vegetable in the world.

John Loudon's Cultivation Advice for 'Practical Men'

When John Claudius Loudon arrived in London at the age of 20 in 1803, he reached the capital during a period of social change that would transform his fortunes – and the contents of the kitchen garden. The Industrial Revolution made many millionaires and the new mercantile class of wealthy industrialists had spawned a generation of amateur gardeners with money to spend. Loudon would help them spend it on their gardens:

'Every man who does not limit the vegetable parts of his dinner to bread and potatoes, is a patron of gardening, by creating a demand for its productions,' he would write later. 'He is a consumer, which is the first species of patron, and the more valuable varieties are such as regularly produce a dessert after dinner, and maintain throughout the year beautiful nosegays and pots of flowers in their lobbies and drawingrooms.'

Loudon had travelled to London meaning to set himself up as a landscape gardener, but he arrived with a letter of recommendation from a professor at Edinburgh University addressed to Sir Joseph Banks. Banks was an eminent man with a botanical knowledge to match the vast library in his Soho Square home. Thirty-five years earlier Banks had sailed with Captain Cook on the *Endeavour*, seen Botany Bay so named, and brought back a raft of new plants. A former scientific adviser to King George, he was now running the botanical gardens at Kew. He was the perfect introduction for the young, ambitious Mr Loudon.

Within a year of meeting Banks, Loudon had written his first book, and over the next forty years, as print costs fell, Loudon wrote for the new, middle-class market. When his books became nineteenth-century best sellers, he founded his *Gardener's Magazine*, one of the early popular gardening periodicals in which he promised to 'record, as they occur, the various discoveries, acquisitions, and improvements that are constantly making in gardening . . . and to render them available to practical men'. Furthermore, wrote the shrewd journalist, his magazine's advertising section would prove just the place to discover where to procure 'paints, cements, manures, compositions for destroying insects such as Davidson's destroyer of earth worms'.

When in 1811 the sale of the lease on his Oxfordshire farm put £15,000 into his pocket, Loudon set off across Europe to find out how foreigners managed their vegetable plots. 'The culinary vegetables of France have not been increased from the earliest period of horticultural history, with the exception of the sea-cale and the potatoe. In salading and legumes they far excel most countries; but in the cabbage tribe, turnips, and potatoes, they are inferior to the moister climates of Holland and Britain.'

Of Russia he wrote: 'the potatoe is but lately introduced, and that only in a few places. Many of the peasants refuse to eat or cultivate this root, from mere prejudice, and from an idea very natural to a people in a state of slavery, that any thing proposed by their lords must be for the lord's advantage, and not theirs; thus the first handful of food thrown to untamed animals operates as a scare.'

THE
GARDENER'S MAGAZINE,

AND REGISTER OF RURAL & DOMESTIC IMPROVEMENT.

GARDENING and GARDENERS For

No. III.
JULY, 1826.

Written for 'gardeners, stewards and others of fixed locality', Loudon's magazine promised to increase their knowledge 'so as to keep pace with the progress of improvements'.

In Italy, things were little better. 'Italian cucumbers are never so succulent as those grown in our humid frames by dung-heat. The love-apple, egg-plant, and capsicum, are extensively cultivated near Rome and Naples for the kitchen; the fruit of the first attaining a larger size, and exhibiting the most grotesque forms. Of culinary vegetables the Italians began with those left them by the Romans, and they added the potatoe to their number as soon as, or before, we did. Though the Italians have the advantage over the rest of Europe in fruits, that good is greatly counterbalanced by the inferiority of their culinary vegetables.'

Loudon never travelled to America, but he gleaned enough details from publications such as seedsman B. McMahon's *American Kalendar* to comment: 'Culinary vegetables grow in the same perfection as in England, excepting the cauliflower and some species of beans. Water-melons, musk-melons, squashes, sweet potatoes, cucumbers, &c. arrive at great perfection.' The growing of squash was of particular interest: 'The seeds of pumpkin are scattered in the field, when planting the corn, and no further trouble is necessary than throwing them into the wagon when ripe.'

John Claudius Loudon died in December 1843. It was the end of an era, but one in which the cause of the common vegetable had been well advanced.

3

Vegetable Husbandry

The Origins of the Kitchen Garden

As necessary to the well-being of a Palestinian household 1,000 years ago as it was to an allotment-holder in Pontefract a century ago, the kitchen garden has a long, if obscure, history. Garden history has tended to celebrate the pleasure grounds and paradise plots of the wealthy not least because they are better documented and lasted longer than those of their lesser yeomen. Yet the antiquity of the kitchen garden is incontestable and many lie, like a host of Heligans in outline, awaiting rediscovery.

It did not help that classical writers stayed largely silent on the subject of the vegetable plot. In medieval times there was a lexicon of Latin, French and English names for garden places including *gardinium, hortus, herbarium, viridium, virgultum* and *vergier*. There was a *wyrtyard*, or little park, and a *herber*, a small ornamental garden with a lawn of less than one acre. The medieval kitchen garden was a *curtilage, leac-garth* or *leac-tun* from the Anglo-Saxon for *geard, tun* or *zeard*, meaning a yard or enclosure – this was the 'backyard' that the Elizabethan settlers carried with them to the Americas.

The common root for the word *giardino* in Italian, *jardin* in French, and *Garten* in German is the Old English *geard* or *garth*, an enclosed place or yard. The first mention of a ketchyngardyn or kechengardyn in Britain appears to be the Bishop of London's manorial accounts of the 1300s. Up until then Europeans kept silent on the subject. The peasant, footstool of the manorial system and mainstay of the medieval economy, had neither the time, skills nor inclination to record anything about his or her methods of growing for the pot. Yet the talents of the peasant gardener ensured that the pottage, a boiled cauldron of vegetables and, occasionally, meat, kept his family alive.

Early European kitchen gardens were little lifelines, fertile plots dedicated to growing the basic necessities. In villages and hamlets across the Continent the kitchen garden hugged the house or stood,

The Anglo-Saxon *leac-garth* evolved into the backyard, a term that Elizabethan settlers then carried with them to the Americas.

encircled by earth banks, ditches and stockades, between the cottages and the fields. On the mirey clays of Burgundy or down on the Somerset levels of western England village gardens were raised up above the flood plain and set upon islands surrounded by drainage dykes and the deep, muddy tracks that marked out their boundaries. Ditches, pools and pig wallows were an intrinsic and practical part of the country scene, since they manured the ground and watered the vegetables. Unfortunately they regularly swallowed up the young too. Bernard Hanawalt in *The Ties that Bound* in 1986 reports that: 'On 29 May 1270 Cicely, aged 2 and a half, went into the yard: a small pig came and tried to take bread from her hand. She fell into a ditch and was drowned.'

Although storable winter staples such as vetches and beans might be sown in strips alongside the orchard where the cutting hay and animal pasture grew, the kitchen garden kept to its conventional 'quarters'. Quartered by a cross of paths, this four-square pattern, edged perhaps with low, clipped hedges of yew, juniper, lavender or dwarf box, was as much part of the kitchen garden scene in ancient Persia as it was to the new Elizabethans of the 1950s growing vegetables in their Surrey suburbs.

Back in Roman times Pliny had already worked out that digging over the 'quarters' of a plot of two-thirds of an acre to a depth of three feet took eight men a day. But we must wait until 820 before some monk saw fit to commit to parchment the design of a European kitchen garden at the Benedictine abbey, Saint-Gall in Switzerland. Here the hortus measured a tenth of an acre and the different esculents were grown in 5.4-metre-long rectangular beds each 6 metres by 1.5 metres wide.

The Benedictine orders (the Black Monks), the later Cistercians (the White Monks) and the Augustinians were as closely wedded to their gardens as they were to their God. Monasteries were centred on the cloistered garth, a patch of grass kept as neat as a bowling green not least because the colour green 'nourishes the eyes and preserves their vision', as one monk would have it. Close by would be the physic garden filled with medicinal plants, a small, locked poison garden, where narcotics such as opium poppies, hemlock and mandrake were grown, and the orchard cemetery, a pleasant place for a burial with its air of quiet contemplation and sanctuary.

Finally there was the utilitarian kitchen or cellarer's garden, run to the very best of his or her abilities by a grumbling friar or nun. St Benedict advised his followers to keep an open house for travellers and to tend the sick and needy. The peasant paid a tax, a tithe or one tenth of his produce, to the clergy. The tax, taken not only from field crops and animals but also from the produce of the 'foot-dug'

The conventional quarters, seen here in a Majorcan garden, have patterned the kitchen garden for centuries.

garden, supported the local monastery, which served as motel, college, roadside diner, citizen advice bureau and hospital, complete with accident and emergency department. Never sure how many guests might be taking bed and board (the board was literally the supper table) and supping at the monastery that evening, the cellarer needed to keep abreast of the latest developments in the cultivation and storage of his esculents.

A cellarer's garden recreated in the monastic gardens of Shrewsbury and designed by Sylvia Landsberg serves to show what the monk Brother Cadfael might have grown. Cadfael, the fictional creation of the late Ellis Peters, was an enthusiastic gardener and herbalist who, like his real ancestors, had gained useful knowledge of the apothecary's art from his travels in the Holy Land. Traditional plots of 1.2-metre-wide beds were surrounded by 0.6-metre paths where coleworts, onions, leeks, leaf beet and broad beans were taken to be eaten green. Nitrogen-restoring legumes were an especially useful crop. Salad, leek and colewort seedlings grew in the nursery bed while the utilitarian fennel, mint, wormwood and hyssop grew nearby. These last were all good 'strewing' plants for spreading on the floors like some medieval air freshener. Cadfael would also have ensured there was a plentiful supply of flax for linen and bandages and hemp for rope and sacking.

The kitchen garden was well stocked. In the 1500s Thomas Tusser lists no less than 1,200 plants for the housewife to grow, and, while his records included medicinal plants, plants for strewing and scenting hand water, and insecticidal plants to keep away the flies, there were plenty of vegetables for the pot. There were brassicas, usually colewort (a kind of kale) and cabbages for the wealthy; parsley, leeks, leaf beet, parsnips, turnips and skirrets; beans and peas, grown to be dried and eaten during the winter; garlic, chives, the 'common bulb onion' and a 'green-leaved one'. In the salad bed the leaves, seeds or petals of a range of self-seeding annuals such as borage, marigold, rocket, feverfew and poppy made as pretty a posy as they did when used to fill the salad bowl.

Around the beginning of the 1500s, when Huguenots fled religious persecution in northern Europe, the English kitchen garden was revitalised. Many Huguenots had lived in the Low Countries, in places like Flanders, where the local gardeners customarily shipped fresh vegetables across the Channel to Britain. Peas imported from Holland were reportedly 'fit dainties for ladies, they come so far, and cost so dear', complained one Mr Fuller. When the Huguenots themselves sailed for England, they brought with them their glass and ropework technologies and their expertise in fruit and vegetable growing. By now herbs and salads, parsley and leaf beet, cucumbers and melons, mint and asparagus (cooked first then eaten cold) were growing happily alongside the onion beds, nursery beds of young plants and beds of medicinal herbs. Beetroot, broad beans, cabbage, lettuce, spinach and turnips, meanwhile, were grown in a system of beds and channels.

When Thomas Hill wrote *The Gardener's Labyrinth* in 1577, he promised to reveal 'worthy Secretes, about the particular sowing and remouing of the moste Kitchen Hearbes; with the wittie ordering of other daintie Hearbes, delectable Floures, pleasant Fruites, and fine Rootes, as the like hath not heretofore bin vttered of any'. Hill advocated trenched beds, with one-foot-wide trenches on either side to water the beds. (This was not to be confused with the practice of 'trenching' or manuring vegetable beds by digging a deep trench and filling the bottom with manure.)

Well-drained paths were laid to separate the vegetable beds from flower borders filled with useful plants such as marigold, ox-eye daisies, carnations and pinks. Intercropping was a useful practice, thought Thomas Hill, with broad beans grown between rows of early potatoes, early dwarf and the later tall peas grown together, and strawberry runners, planted between rows of onions, being left to grow on for harvesting the following year, after the onions had been lifted.

The kitchen garden, like the formal flower garden, was kept neat. Seed was sown in drills rather than broadcast or sown in patches. For the fastidious kitchen gardener there was the practice of quincunx, a method of 'planting in rows, by which the plants in the one row are always opposed to the blanks in the other, so that when a plot of ground is planted in this way, the plants appear in rows in four directions'.

For the time being the gardener's choice of vegetables was based upon what had been passed down from the Persians, Greeks, Romans, Christians and Christian academics – universities like Toledo, Cordoba, Bologna and Paris had all furthered the development of vegetables, as had the great botanical gardens of Pisa, Padua, Parma and Florence. But the growing two-way trade with America was about to bring about an unparalleled transformation in the vegetable patch.

In America intercropping and companion planting was a well-established craft in the communal gardens of the native Americans. Corn was sown, after due ceremony and respectful rituals, and fertilised with whatever was available locally, whether it was fish and wood ash or bat dung from neighbouring caves. Corn was followed by lima and kidney or pinto beans, the beans using the stems of the maize for support. Then it was the turn of the pumpkins, squashes and sunflowers (for oil) and Jerusalem artichokes (for their storable tubers). The ripening of the first cobs of corn was a cause for celebration and the cobs would be baked in the embers of the fire at the Green Corn Festival. Mature cobs from the later crops would be hung in ropes like strings of onions and stored in the smoky rafters of the Indian lodge.

The early European settlers were suspicious at first of South America's maize, potatoes, tomatoes, peppers and yams and North America's marrows, squash, pumpkins, Jerusalem artichokes and beans. But once they and their families had been rescued from extinction by these native American crops, they extolled their vegetable virtues and sent the seed home to Europe. It was put to good use. Indian maize was so nutritious that it was said to be responsible for doubling the population of Spain in the 1700s. The potato did the same for the half-starved Irish people, whose population rose from three million in 1750 to eight million in 1845 before potato blight triggered the disastrous crop failures.

In the Industrial Age the kitchen garden underwent more radical reforms. Working men grew essential supplies on their allotments; the 'villa' gardener devoted the bottom of the garden to vegetables, while the aristocracy poured thousands of pounds into prestigious and productive fruit and vegetable gardens. Snobbery was rife – even in the kitchen garden. 'Let us begin with the earliest crops (of peas) which the cottagers seldom aims at; but which the gentleman's gardener and the amateur must produce, so as to have them on the table long before poor people think of such a thing,' wrote the Victorian gardener Shirley Hibberd. The cottager, amateur and gentleman's gardener, who was generally a cottager in his spare time anyway and perfectly capable of raising early peas if he chose, might have every conceivable vegetable at his disposal, but he still had to contend with the seasons. The methods taken to defeat the seasons marked the next significant change.

While market growers in the vales of Kent and Evesham concentrated on mass production, research and development fell to those earnest amateurs on their country estates, aided by armies of gardeners. It was no use relying on 'Johnny Foreigner': 'Horticulture has made little progress in Italy. Forcing or prolonging crops is unknown; everything is sown at a certain season, and grows up, ripens, and perishes together. The red and white beet, salsify, scorzonera, chervile, sorrel, onion, schallot, Jerusalem artichoke, are in many parts unknown,' declared Loudon.

It was left to the estate head gardeners to forward vegetable development, exchanging ideas and sharing their knowledge in popular publications such as *Gardener's Magazine, Gardeners' Chronicle* and the *Journal of Horticulture and Cottage Gardening*.

Technological developments in iron and glass making, and the advancing science of the heating engineer, gave the Victorians the means to grow any and every vegetable – and send them to the table at almost any time of year. All that was required was money and manpower. However, the rumble of cannon fire on the fields of

The great vegetable gardens with their acres of glasshouses went into steep decline after the Second World War.

Flanders was about to bring it all to an end. The Duke of Devonshire's 400-year-old estate at Chatsworth in Derbyshire was a case in point. The great house was provisioned by a seven-acre kitchen garden and, by 1905, with almost two acres of glass housing. No less than forty-six gardeners posed for their photograph before the Great Conservatory in 1890. But by 1917 their numbers were halved. Shortly after the end of the First World War the greenhouses were sold off and plans were drawn up to discontinue the kitchen garden altogether. Death duties, labour costs and, finally, the Second World War would see the greengrocer rather than the gardener provisioning these palaces of the Edwardian and Victorian age.

For the rest of the population, however, urbanisation and the industrial age had reduced city gardens to a fraction of their former selves. There was a saccharine nostalgia for old cottage gardens where radishes and runner beans grew among the roses. Amateur gardeners were still cropping vegetables where they could, on allotments or pinched plots of waste land. People wanted gardens.

A copy-writer for Sutton's seed catalogue of 1881 warned: 'We are bound to keep in mind that the system is unsound which permits increase of houses without a corresponding multiplication of gardens.'

On the eve of the 1900s a parliamentary reporter and inventor, Ebenezer Howard, gave voice to these aspirations. Living in the country, he pointed out, brought 'Beauty of Nature, Bright Sunshine and Abundance of Water', but it was blighted by 'Lack of Society, Trespassers Beware and Deserted Spirit'. In town the benefits of 'Opportunity, High Money Wages and Places of amusement' had to be offset against 'Closing Out of Nature, Foul Air, High Rents, and Slums and Palaces'. The perfect compromise, argued Howard, was a 'garden city', a place that combined town and country and that boasted 'Beauty of Nature, Social Opportunity, and Fields and Parks of Easy Access, and Homes and Gardens'. Howard's reforming ideas paved the way for an era of social housing, gardens and vegetable plots for all. Benevolent industrialists including William Lever at Port Sunlight on Merseyside and George Cadbury at Bournville in Birmingham had already provided vegetable allotments with their workers' homes. Now garden towns modelled on Howard's theories were built at Letchworth from 1903 and Welwyn from 1920. Howard's homes, each with a garden and a vegetable plot, formed a template for housing estates right through the twentieth century, although, after the wartime frenzy of vegetable growing, the vegetable plot began to retreat down the gardens. The preserving and packaging industries and the availability of cheap imported vegetables made store-bought produce cheap and attractive.

Then, just as Stuart Dudley was suggesting in the 1960s that it was 'uneconomical in the accepted meaning of the word to keep the kitchen supplied with vegetables from the garden', the kitchen garden started to enjoy a slow revival.

There was a whole-food movement and a rise in vegetarianism in the 1960s. In the 1970s students grew vegetables among their cannabis plants on dubious pieces of squatted ground, and hippies, in between protests against the Vietnam War, took over unloved allotments to grow fresh vegetables to accompany their frugal meals of brown rice and bacon bits. There were fastidious biodynamic gardeners and organic growers who, frustrated in their search for pesticide-free produce, turned to growing their own. There were city farms and social projects espousing the therapeutic

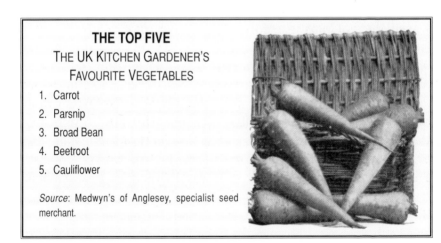

THE TOP FIVE
THE UK KITCHEN GARDENER'S
FAVOURITE VEGETABLES

1. Carrot
2. Parsnip
3. Broad Bean
4. Beetroot
5. Cauliflower

Source: Medwyn's of Anglesey, specialist seed merchant.

benefits of growing vegetables for people with disabilities. Television, which was overtaking gardening as one of the nation's most popular pastimes, played its part by creating improbable media celebrities of gardeners like Geoff Hamilton who were more than happy to show a nation how to grow vegetables again. In 1999 the prestigious garden exhibition at Chaumont-sur-Loire was devoted to 'Nothing but Vegetables', and, as rock stars like Paul and Linda McCartney, *avant-garde* artists like Jacqueline de Jong and even royals like the Prince of Wales reinstated their vegetable gardens, home-grown vegetables once again became as fashionable as they were fresh.

Boundaries, Walls and Fences

Good fences make good neighbours. They also make good kitchen gardens. The need to fence the vegetable plot has exercised gardeners for centuries. Hedges, sunken fences, walls and wide water courses all played their part.

Water was an effective way to keep predators off the kitchen garden. (It could keep them in too; in medieval times a water-filled ditch was often used to contain the rabbit warren and ensure a supply of fresh meat.) A ready water supply also allowed for regular watering and a place to grow useful willows, rushes and watermint.

In pre-Roman Britain, at least, there was no need to fret about rabbit fencing since the coney had yet to be brought to Britain by the Romans, but there were other beasts to worry about before, and after, the Roman invasion. A surplus of wolves and rioting Welshmen drove the monks of Llanthony Priory from their monastery in the remote Black Mountains of Wales to the safety of Gloucester in 1135. Once the wolves were gone, marauding deer and cattle might still devour the peasant's winter supplies of leeks

Coping with adversity and wolves – the Augustinian monks at Llanthony Priory in Wales were cultivating their vegetables nine centuries ago.

and coleworts. While the peasant was pestered by rapacious animals, abbots and abbesses fretted about light-fingered passers-by. Stone walls were usefully employed to guard the vegetable plot. The oldest dated wall in Britain, at Skara Brae on Orkney, was built around 1500 BCE, while the silvered stone boundaries that criss-cross the limestone uplands of Britain were infants by comparison, many dating back to the monastic wool trade of the 1200s and 1300s. The golden limestone walls of the Cotswolds gardens were later additions still. Most date back to the Enclosure Acts of the 1700s and 1800s.

The waller's craft varied from region to region, those using Cotswold stone topping their walls with combers while wallers in the Peak District had a preference for upright coping stones laid in a 'cock and hens' style. The Cornishman, meanwhile, favoured an earthen bank reinforced with a herringbone pattern of stone.

Emperor Caesar, pushing through northern Europe during the Gallic Wars, was impressed by a different type of boundary, the hedge. 'These hedges present a barrier like a wall,' he wrote. The living hedge, protected by a ditch to keep browsing cattle at bay, was made by planting saplings of thorn, oak, crab, hawthorn and holly against a temporary stake and pole fence. Within a decade the saplings were tall enough to be laid, when the sap was down, during the winter. The hedger would cut into the lower part of the sapling and, bending it over, weave it around fresh stakes cut from surplus hedge timber. The top of the hedge was finished with a whippy rail of willow or hazel and a small willow bed was often planted close by to provide spare parts. As Thomas Tusser pointed out in his *Five Hundred Pointes of Good Husbandrie* in 1573:

> euerie [every] hedge
> hath plenty of fewell and fruit.

Good fences, such as this bullock-proof barricade in Estonia, make good neighbours and keep predators out of the kitchen garden.

Anyone caught stealing that 'fewell' faced being whipped until they 'bled well' for the offence of hedgebreaking and to compensate the landowner, who would have to call on the hedgemender to make good the damage. (The hedgemender was said to be pictured as the man on the moon, a dim-witted individual carrying a forkload of thorns on his back to repair a hedge.)

A dead hedge was an acceptable alternative to the living hedge. In Estonia, tall hazel rods, or ethers, as they were called in sixteenth-century England, were woven between three horizontal poles; in Sweden, pine poles, held together with a twist of bark, rested at 45 degrees in a timber framework; in north and west Wales, fangs of slate, waste from the quarries, were stood on end and wired together in a crude imitation of the picket or paling fence (a pale from the

Latin *palus*, a stake). This boundary fence, so cherished by suburban America, has interesting antecedents. The primary purpose of the 'pale' in the Middle Ages was not to protect the kitchen garden, but to keep fallow deer in their proper place – the nobleman's park. The medieval pale was made of split or cleft oak stakes set in the ground and nailed to horizontal rails, and, to make doubly sure the deer stayed in, a bank and ditch were added, the pale fence being run along the top of the bank. (In Ireland, after the conquest of Henry II, the English settled within 'The Pale', an area fenced off against the Irish. Those living 'beyond the pale' were beyond redemption.)

Once the gardener had enclosed his growing plot with hedge, fence or wall, he soon realised an unexpected benefit: a walled garden is a warm garden. By the time of Queen Victoria's coronation in 1837, the walled kitchen garden was a fashionable favourite, not least because the brick wall raised the temperature within the garden by a degree or two. A century later, without the workforce required to tend them, these kitchen gardens were crumbling into disrepair. Another half a century on and campaigners were calling for their restoration.

Within the walled garden, the conventional square- or rectangular-shaped garden was traditionally quartered by four vegetable plots surrounded by paths and wall-side borders. Their dimensions reflected the size of the household: at Holkham in Norfolk, for example, the walls enclosed no less than six acres. Walled gardens were oriented slightly to the west of south so that the heat of the early afternoon was concentrated on one wall. This suntrap wall, which stored the heat and released it through the chill night, was usually built higher than the other walls so as to make the most of its position. It was a fine site for fruit: figs, vines, peaches, apricots and nectarines would be planted against the south-west walls and late fruiting plums, gooseberries, currants and morello cherries against the north wall.

The garden designer Humphry Repton liked to design walled gardens with six or seven sides, while the gardening author William Robinson built his walled garden at Gravetye, Sussex, in an oval shape. He used dressed stone rather than brick because, he believed, the stone's smooth surface afforded fewer hiding places for insects. In the USA Thomas Jefferson built a serpentine wall around his garden at Monticello in the late 1700s: rounded or crinkle-crankle walls, also known as *slangenmuren* or snake walls, were popular briefly in the UK in the late 1700s and early 1800s. The additional wall surface provided extra surface for heating – one garden writer advocated covering the walls in metal to reflect the heat into the garden, although there is no evidence that his suggestion was ever put into practice. But in 1755 Thomas Hitt dismissed the serpentine walls as 'attended with evils of one kind or other. Though walls built with curves have, in calm seasons, the benefit of more heat than others; yet, in windy weather, the winds . . . rebounding from side to side, break and destroy the tender branches and blossoms of trees.'

Fires might be lit inside the walled garden to counter frosts; they were even lit beneath the soil to force fruit, but a more effective way to raise the temperature or limit frost damage was to heat the walls themselves. Hot or flued walls were used in kitchen gardens from the mid-1700s, the telltale signs being the small cast-iron doors or framed stones set in the wall to clean out the flues. Flues in some walls, however, were simply made large enough for chimney sweeps' children to climb in and clean, while at Fonthill, in Wiltshire, the work was carried out, allegedly, by the estate's Jamaican dwarves. Heated walls were eventually superseded by heated glasshouses built against the walls.

Being fire-resistant, cheap and attractive, brick was judged the ideal walling material, although other materials included cob, pisé, chalk, timber and even plate glass mounted on iron frames.

The atmosphere in a walled garden is like that of a church, says former gardener Keith Ruck. 'You got to show a bit of reverence.'

Temporary timber walls were another alternative, one design involving timber walls made of deal planks against which were heaped middens of hot manure. They were so successful, according to one commentator, that the kitchen gardener could raise 'gooseberries fit for tarts' in January. But dark-red, well-fired (and therefore harder and longer lasting) brick was judged best. The introduction of a tax on bricks in 1750 slowed the pace of walled-garden construction, but by 1850, when the tax was repealed, the demands of the country-house guests on the produce of the vegetable garden made the walled kitchen garden as necessary as a polite parlour maid and a deferential butler.

Although the twentieth century saw the walled garden spiral into a near terminal decline, organisations such the Walled Gardens Network were formed to save and preserve the remainder. It was a feature worthy of conservation if the recol-lections of West Midlands head gardener Keith Ruck were anything to go by: 'There's something about working in a walled garden. The atmosphere is like working in a church: I always remember when the gardens were open and you'd be down there and there'd be hundreds of people milling round. Then, at dusk when they'd gone home and you'd go down to shut some lights up or something, you'd turn in the doorway when you was coming out from there and it almost feels like you got to shut the door quietly. I've heard other old gardeners say the same: you almost think like you got to show a bit of reverence.'

Muck and Magic

How do you grow good vegetables? The answer, as the BBC radio comedian Kenneth Williams used to say, lies in the soil. That soil had to be constantly improved and manure was the essential improver.

A Good Idea at the Time
Monkey Muck

The nineteenth-century mania for finding garden fertiliser led trading ships to the Lacapede Islands, off the remote north-west coast of Australia, in the late 1800s. Here millions of nesting sea birds had created mountains of droppings. The guano, as it was known, was a rich source of fertiliser, and, despite the dangers of these territorial waters – ten ships were shipwrecked in 1877 – the guano was mined and exported across the world. The bird droppings proved so profitable that the Americans decided to claim the islands for their own, erecting the Stars and Stripes on the island and sparking an international incident. The Western Australian Government was forced to station a representative on the lonely islands to reclaim them for Australia. Eventually the guano, sometimes referred to as 'monkey muck', ran out.

'Be avaricious for manure, and always keep your mind in firm conviction that your ground is in an impoverished state,' advised Shirley Hibberd. A comprehensive list of manures from the early 1800s included sea weed, spoiled hay, tanner's spent bark, Cornish pilchards and Fenland sticklebacks, whale blubber ('good reports from Surrey'), horn and bone, hair, woollen rags, blood, coral, urine,

Droppings from inside the dovecote, one of the 'finest activator manures of all', according to Lawrence D. Hills, would sweeten the vegetable soil.

pigeon dung and the dung of domestic fowls, cattle, oxen, sheep, deer and camels, street and road dung, soot, soapers' waste and house sweepings. One Mr Young reported an experiment where a field was spread with herrings and ploughed in for wheat. The crop, however, was 'so rank' it was 'laid before harvest'.

The use of street sweepings continued into the 1920s and 1930s, as gardener Keith Ruck recalled. 'In those days around Abergavenny they had the linesman, as they was called, and they used to cut the sides of the road: put the line down and no twists and all done perfect there. The leaves were all swept up and then all that was put in tumps along the side of the road. Some of the farmers had horse and carts under contract to the council for collecting it up. We used to get them to tip it near the bottom of the garden. Then, when that was rotted, we used to sieve it all out and use it for a seed compost.'

For a liquid feed Mr Ruck senior would take an old tar barrel, burn out the remaining tar and fill it with water. 'We used to scrounge round all the farms for when the farmers were dagging, that was cleaning the rear ends of lambs and sheep before shearing. We used to collect all those, put 'em in a hessian sack and hang them in the barrel. That was our liquid feed. You couldn't beat it.'

For solid manuring, the vegetable garden was double dug or trenched, a method that involved digging a trench two spits of a spade deep, laying the bottom of the trench with well-rotted manure and covering the trench with soil excavated from the next row along. A bed might be trenched every four or five years. Some writers, possibly those who could pay the gardener to do it for them, advocated a back-breaking trench three spits deep.

Another way to keep the ground in good heart was to leave a plot fallow for a year. The term fallow, as in fallow deer, referred to the pale red or pale yellow colour of land that had been turned or ploughed, but left unsown.

Apart from perennials such as Jerusalem artichokes or asparagus, most vegetables in the northern hemisphere were planted in spring. Half of the crops – onions, peas, beans and salads – was harvested within six months, and the remainder over the rest of the year. A rule of thumb to avoid the ground 'getting tired' was never to follow a crop with another of the same family. 'A studied rotation is advisable. The kitchen garden should be divided into a number of portions, and a journal or notebook should be kept, with a reference to their numbers,' advised a head gardener, Mr Nicol, in his *Kitchen Gardener* of 1802.

Through the 1900s the more intensive four-crop rotation saw potatoes, legumes, brassicas and roots trooping after one another around the plots. Heavy manuring and deep digging for the potato crop benefited the beans and peas that followed. Their nitrogen-fixing roots aided the growth of the brassicas, while the final root crop would grow straight and true. In his classic *Organic Gardening* (1977) Lawrence D. Hills advocated a four-crop rotation with four beds to fit into a standard allotment or 'two beds, one on each side of the centre path of the average 1930s-built semi-detached house garden'. His practical description evokes the suburban back garden with its 'cropping space, bush fruit, herb bed near the kitchen door, tool shed and compost bin behind the garage, and the lawn crossed by the clothes line'.

Back in medieval times, while every good gardener knew how to fertilise the soil, they were hard pressed to explain the process. Cardinal Nicolas of Cusa, who weighed soil and plant before and after the crop matured, discovered that the soil's weight had altered little. Water, he concluded, played a significant part in the process.

In the 1200s scientists at the University of Bologna experimented with seeds and plants in the hope that their discovery might lead to their being able to turn base metals into gold. The secret of soil fertility was still something of a holy grail for the alchemists of the 1500s and 1600s. The Germans were first past the post when, in the mid-1800s, Justus von Liebig revealed that plants took in carbonic acid, water, ammonia, potassium, calcium, magnesium, phosphate and sulphate, converting them into starch, sugar, fat and proteins. Furthermore, he confirmed that animals, which ate and excreted plants, returned these elements to the soil. He was nearly, but not quite there, and it fell to the German botanist Julius Sachs to identify the essential minerals. His list did not include the actual soil and in 1860 he astonished the horticultural world by growing plants hydroponically in mineral-fed water.

Then, after two German chemists studying sugar beet had discovered how plants take up nitrogen, John Bennet Lawes and Joseph Gilbert working at Lawes's family home, Rothamsted Manor in Hertfordshire, devised the ingredients for an artificial fertiliser. Within half a century gardeners were producing remarkable results with their new chemicals: nitrate of soda, nitrate of potash or sulphate of ammonia, sulphate of potash, superphosphate of lime. Potash developed the sugars and starches in potatoes and tomatoes especially, while nitrogen inputs were fast working and produced vigorous green plants. But there was a spectre on the horizon. When scientists revealed that the once useful pesticide Dichloro-

The well-managed compost heap could restore soil fertility and put essential minerals back into the ground.

diphenyl-trichloroethane or DDT had entered the global food chain, vegetable gardeners began to wonder what they were doing to their soils – and to themselves. The garden world was becoming a potentially poisonous place with residuals such as antibiotics, copper, pesticides, herbicides, cadmium and lead lurking in modern manures and composts. The indications were that the high productivity produced by chemical fertilisers and fearsome pesticides in the kitchen garden could prove to be environmentally damaging. Many turned to the organic lobby and the prophet of the new organic age, Lawrence Hills.

In the 1970s, with high inflation and the cost of food rising, Hills predicted that many would be forced to try for self-sufficiency, 'as peasants do in many countries. With skilled gardening and a rotation that crops through the winter, the 300 square yards of the standard allotment can produce nearly a ton and a half of food in a year,' he declared. There were plenty of people ready to try. Their first task was to master the mysteries of the compost heap.

The Compost Heap

While sailors and climbers have their knots, truck drivers and travelling salespeople their preferred routes from A to B, vegetable gardeners have their compost heaps. 'You have one source of the very best manure in the household, and you must treasure every scrap of stinking rubbish, solid and liquid, and not waste so much as a dead cabbage leaf,' trumpeted Shirley Hibberd. It was not a new idea. In the 1800s gardeners had collected highway manure, grass, weeds, mud from ditches, leaves, soot ashes, and household refuse, mixing them together 'in the dunghill, and turned frequently over before using'.

A Ministry of Agriculture approved design for a Second World War compost heap.

A century later the wartime gardener Arthur J. Simons, writing in 1941 (though published later) was reminding readers of *The Vegetable Grower's Handbook*: 'The increasing shortage of stable manure, arising out of the decay of horse transport and the difficulty of obtaining any kind of animal manure in and around towns . . . have combined to encourage the conversion of vegetable waste of the garden into manure by the making of compost heaps.' He went on to describe no less than six different methods of making a compost, including the Indore process and the 'Quick Return'.

The key to the fermentation of a compost heap made of vegetable matter, soil, water and air was the presence of nitrogen, which acted as a starter and accelerated the digestion of material into humus. Dung, rich in phosphates, and urine, rich in nitrogen and potash, were powerful activators. The best dung, insisted the Muslim gardeners of Spain in the 1400s, came from the best animals: the manure of a corn-fed stallion was infinitely preferable to that of the tired pack horse grazed on poor hay. Top of the list was bird dung, not least because the dung and urine were so neatly packaged into one dropping. Journals from St Peter's in Gloucester record that the mountains of dove droppings from inside the dovecote or columbaria were shovelled out on to the garden twice a year. And there was no point in wasting good urine: in the 1300s Ibn Bassâl (or Bassal) advised that labourers be encouraged to urinate on the compost. The Roman Columella commended human urine especially if it was to be stored for six months and mixed with 'old oil lees' before being applied to the olive crop.

In his *Organic Gardening* (1977) Lawrence Hills listed his top eight manure producers from horse, cow and pig to goat, chicken, rabbit and pigeon. 'Goat manure is perhaps the best general manure of the lot, because the goat is a browser rather than a grazer . . . but the finest activator manure of all is pigeon droppings.'

Waste not, want not. The products of the earth closet would fire up the compost heap.

Until the unveiling of the latest design for the water closet at the Great Exhibition of 1851, the vegetable soil was regularly 'sweetened' by the products of the privy. King Henry III ordered 'a privy chamber to the Queen's *garderobe*' in 1296. The *garderobe*, the French word for a small chamber for storing clothes, became, in the Middle Ages, the polite term for what was later called euphemistically the smallest room.

In 1941 Arthur J. Simons was recommending adding night soil to the compost list. 'Night' soil (soil was from the French *souiller* to sully or defile) referred to the practice of emptying the earth closet at night: 'About once a year a Negro we called Mister Elsey would come with his wagon and clean the vault of our privy,' recalled an American Carl Sandburg in John Pudney's *The Smallest Room* (1954). 'His work was always done at night. He came and went like a shadow in the moon.'

In England in the Middle Ages it was the work of the gong fermors (gong meaning a privy and fermors from the verb 'fey', to cleanse).

Through the 1600s, 1700s and 1800s, there was a running battle over how long such manure should be allowed to 'ferment' before it was dug into the kitchen garden. In the 1800s 'desiccated night-soil' was sold in France as *poudrette*. In London, it was mixed with quicklime and sold in cakes under the name Clarke's Desiccated Compost. The Chinese, too, were said to 'have more practical knowledge of the use of manures than any other people existing', and mixed their night soil with earth and fashioned it into saleable cakes.

Various attempts were made to mechanise the process of making manure safe for the vegetable plot. In 1860 Moule's Earth-Closet Company patented the Revd Henry Moule's device for automatically discharging a quantity of dry earth into the latrine when pressure was exerted on the lavatory seat. Sales were slow, because the contraption required a plentiful supply of dry, finely sifted earth: ensuring a supply meant purchasing a special earth drying and sifting stove for the purpose.

The Revd Moule, had he any children, would, like others of his class, expect the morning maid to empty the chamber pots daily on to the garden compost heap. The compost heap was, and still is, the ideal way to return to the soil as much organic matter as possible. The decomposing vegetation was home to millions of soil organisms that fed the soil, improved drainage on heavy soils and helped retain water on light soils. With or without *poudrette*, it was judged to be a horticultural wonder.

John Innes's Revolutionary Potting Composts

John Innes is to the garden what the Hoover is to the home, thanks to the potting compost that bears his name. Born in 1829, Innes became a successful London property developer and land dealer. When he died in 1904 he left £325,000 to set up a horticultural research centre. The John Innes Horticultural Institute opened in Surrey, and was moved later to Norwich in Norfolk. Contrary to popular belief, the institute never produced a gram of commercial potting composts – but it did invent the first successful formula.

It had been common for gardeners to rely on their own recipes for soils in which to grow seeds, slips and cuttings. A Mr Cushing who worked at a nursery in Hammersmith, London, in 1812 divulged his own formula to the readers of *Exotic Garden*: 'Loam, peat, and sand, seem to be the three simples of nature, if I may so call them, most requisite for our purpose; to which we occasionally add as mollifiers, vegetable or leaf mould, and well rotted dung; for the judicious mixture and preparation of which, composts may be made to suit plants introduced from any quarter of the globe.'

Sometimes these composts were sterilised, but more often they were not, and the gardener's stock might be summarily destroyed by a soil-borne disease. Too much fertiliser added to the compost caused the plants to grow leggy and 'soft' or weak; too little and they grew 'hard' or slow growing.

The John Innes composts, based on a mix of seven parts of soil or loam, three parts of peat and two of grit, were devised in the 1930s. They were the work of two researchers at the institute, William Lawrence and John Newell. Lawrence and Newell had been frustrated in their efforts to grow standard Chinese primroses (*Primula sinensis*) for research purposes because of the lack of a standard compost. In the end they devoted six years to perfecting two standard composts, one for seed sowing and one for potting.

The John Innes Number 1, for sowing seed, rooting soft cuttings and pricking out or potting up young seedlings or rooted cuttings, carried only a small amount of nutrients. Number 2, for the general potting of vegetable plants and house plants into medium-sized pots or boxes, contained double the amount of fertiliser. The nutrients, nitrogen for top growth, phosphates for root growth, potash for flowering and fruiting, and trace elements for colour and flavour, were perfectly balanced. The basic ingredient, loam, was made from rotted-down, stacked turf, which was sterilised before being added to sphagnum moss peat and coarse sand or grit to provide the right amount of drainage.

Later John Innes Number 3 was introduced with a richer mixture for final repotting of heavier feeding vegetables such as cucumbers and tomatoes, and mature plants and shrubs in interior planters or outdoor containers.

The composts became an industry standard and revolutionised the growing of seeds and plants in pots. Fifty years later, although the nutrients had changed, the basic formula remained the same.

The Findhorn Secret: Growth and Sensibility

To be 'a vegetable' is to lack sensibility. Aristotle accepted that vegetables had no sensations, but, he insisted, they did possess souls. In the 1900s a Viennese biologist, Raol Francé, declared that not only did vegetables and other plants move about freely, although on a time scale too slow for us to follow; they were also highly sensitive to either abuse or gratitude. Authors such as Peter Tompkins and Christopher Bird, in their *The Secret Life of Plants* (1975) celebrated the sensibility of sunflowers, which turned, like incautious sunbathers, to face the sun as it travelled from east to west (hence their French name *tour de sol* and Italian *girasol*). 'Plants may . . . be the bridesmaids at a marriage of physics and metaphysics,' suggested the authors. Three extraordinary vegetable-growers were about to reveal that plants had allies in the spirit world.

They were an ex-Royal Air Force squadron leader, Peter Caddy, his wife Eileen and their friend Dorothy MacLean. The three had been running the Cluny Hotel in Scotland during the 1950s, when they embarked upon a major life change. Moving to a scruffy caravan site in a remote part of north Scotland that looked out across Findhorn Bay, they were determined to turn away from the materialistic world and pursue a life of 'limitless love and truth'. Central to their aspirations was the raising of vegetables.

There are diminishing returns to be had from most vegetables the further north you travel. Shorter growing seasons and fewer growing days, earlier and later frosts, and poor or indifferent soils all play a part. Peter Caddy found the soil at Findhorn as 'fine, dusty sand and gravel in which nothing grew but rough pointed grass'. Nevertheless he double dug the plot, laying the upturned turves at the bottom of the trench and erected a wind-proof fence, recycled from a dismantled garage. The land was manured with seaweed and the produce of the compost heap. The women, meanwhile, sought spiritual guidance. Eileen, who had renamed herself Elixir, spoke of her midnight meditations and her vision of the rundown caravan park transformed into a place with seven cedar-wood bungalows. Dorothy became Divina.

In their first year Divina, Elixir and the more prosaic Peter harvested onions, leeks, garlic, carrot, parsnip, swede, turnip, artichoke, kohlrabi, celery, marrow, potatoes, over twenty different kinds of salad and various herbs. In the autumn they pickled 6.75 kilograms of red cabbage, bottled cucumbers and put potatoes, carrots, beetroot, shallot, onion and garlic in store for the winter. In 1964 Peter Caddy grew a cabbage that weighed 20.25 kilograms. A single sprouting broccoli fed the group for weeks and was said to be too heavy to lift.

When Sir George Trevelyan, a leading member of the Soil Association and doyen of the New Age, visited the site, he was amazed at the fertility, growth and taste of the vegetables. Peter Caddy revealed the Findhorn secret: Divina had made spiritual contact with whole hierarchies of plant spirits, or devas, who instructed her on how to make the most of the vegetables. She expounded on the theory that you are what you eat, explaining that plants fed the soul as well as the body: vegetables grown by a bad-tempered gardener, for example, could themselves cause ill humour in those who ate them. 'You are perfectly free to say this is nonsense,' Trevelyan would later say in an interview. 'Here you are in the middle of the twentieth century and we're talking of fairies in your garden. But how else do you explain the plants that grow on these decayed sand dunes?'

Within ten years Elixir's premonitions were fulfilled. Findhorn went on to become an established community of 300 people, wealthy enough to buy up the caravan park and replace the caravans with the seven cedar-wood bungalows predicted by Elixir. Even the old Cluny Hill Hotel, as well as neighbouring properties, were purchased to house the expanding educational charity of Findhorn. The Findhorn vegetables had proved to be a strange success.

Rudolph Steiner's Biodynamic Vegetables

In 1982 the retiring Director of Agriculture for Tanganyika wrote a book called *Biodynamic Gardening* (published in 1995). John Soper had been a dutiful servant of the British colonial service. He had spent thirty-two years in East Africa and Malaya. Captured by the Japanese during the Second World War, he was a prisoner of war for three and a half years. In his retirement he was to promote some unorthodox ideas on vegetable husbandry.

'More and more people today', he wrote, 'are convinced in their heart that the world which we see and hear around us is not the

Grain being harvested on land owned by a UK insurance company. Rudolph Steiner's biodynamic vegetable-growing methods arose from concerns over twentieth-century farming practices.

only one; behind it and beyond the range of our senses there must be other worlds which underlie, inform, permeate and organise all our national surroundings.'

When Soper retired to work his vegetable and fruit patch, first in Hampshire and later at Clent, near Birmingham, he became a leading member of the Biodynamic Association, a movement founded on the teachings of Rudolph Steiner.

Steiner, the son of an Austrian station master, was born in 1861 and died in 1925. By the age of 8 he had already experienced 'the reality of the spiritual world'. In his forties he was devoting himself to the 'science of the spirit', or what he called anthroposophy. His writings and teachings founded the Camphill villages, devoted to the care of people with learning disabilities, and Waldorf schools as well as methods of biodynamic farming and gardening.

In the 1920s Steiner's supporters were as concerned about agricultural trends as consumers were in the 1980s, and, when he presented a series of lectures on farming in 1924, his ideas on agriculture were adapted to form the basis of biodynamic vegetable gardening. Even ardent followers like Soper, however, found Steiner's notions difficult to follow: 'He emphasised that he was speaking from his personal experience on small peasant farms, and he did not mention gardens at all,' wrote Soper later. Nevertheless the biodynamic movement, based at Goetheanum in Dornach, Switzerland, has become a global influence on vegetable-growers.

'The earth breathes, it has a respiratory system, it has a pulse, it is sensitive and it has a skin,' explained Soper. Break the skin with a cutting or landslide and it would heal itself in time with a protective layer of vegetation. The earthly life form expanded and contracted like any breathing being, said Soper. He suggested that the gardener work in harmony with its rhythms, harvesting leaf vegetables and transplanting seedlings in the expanding mornings, for example, and sowing seeds, harvesting root crops and transplanting small plants during the evenings as the earth gently contracted.

Equally important to the growth of vegetables was the influence of the planetary rhythms. The parts of the plant – root, leaf, flower and fruit – mirrored the four elements – earth, water, air and light, and fire – and all came under the influence of the moon, sun and the zodiac, that ring of twelve constellations against which the sun appears to move in the course of a year. Esoteric perhaps, but Soper pointed out how vegetables in the northern hemisphere grew to their climax as the sun drove on towards its summer solstice and then waned and ripened as it headed towards the autumn equinox. The moon, he argued, was a mighty influence.

'Most authorities agreed that seed should be sown with a waxing moon,' insisted one writer in the 1800s. Native Americans sensibly looked for the star cluster Pleiades, or the Seven Sisters, to disappear from the spring sky before planting their seed, since this signalled the beginning of frost-free nights. The Roman Paracelsus wrote of the moon's influence on plants and 2,000 years later one Cornish head gardener, R.J. Harris, attributed his success at vegetable growing to following the four quarters of the moon. He was echoing the advice of John Worlidge, who, in 1669, advocated regulating the performance of horticultural operations by the age of the moon. Worlidge declared that turnips or onions, sown when the moon was full, would not 'bulb out', but send up flower stalks instead. A weak tree, he added, should be pruned as the moon waxed and a strong one as it waned.

In 1693 the French author of *The Complete Gardener*, Jean-Baptiste de La Quintinye, dismissed the theory. 'I solemnly declare that after a diligent observation of the moon's changes for thirty years together, and an enquiry whether they had any influence in gardening, the affirmative of which has been so long established among us, I perceived that it was no weightier than old wives' tales, and that it had been advanced by unexperienced gardeners. Sow what sorts of grains you please, and plant as you please, in any quarter of the moon, I'll answer for your success, the first and last day of the moon being equally favourable.'

In the early 1800s Loudon, too, dismissed the lunar influence as 'superstitious observances attendant on a rude state of society'. But John Soper held to his view that plants that bore their crops above ground would grow better when sown during a waxing moon while root crops would thrive when sown as the moon waned.

The biodynamic gardener had first to familiarise himself with his soil, taking a fistful of moist earth and squeezing it into a lump. A sandy soil would fall apart, a clay soil form into a lumpy ball. A second test involved mixing a soil sample with water in a glass jar, shaking it up and allowing it to settle. Sand would fall to the bottom while clay formed a sludgelike mix at the top. Having established the nature of his soil, the biodynamic gardener could cultivate it with respect, because, on planet earth, every gardener and every garden was an individual. Deep digging and trenching were reserved for heavy clay soils, while light, sandy soils required little cultivation and benefited from being sheltered from the elements with a cover crop of weeds when it lay fallow.

Horticultural pesticides and artificial fertilisers were to be avoided: 'One fact does appear to be fairly certain,' wrote Soper. 'The effects are partially or wholly negatived by the use of artificial fertilisers and agricultural poisons which deaden the soil's sensitivity and responsiveness.' Instead, the biodynamic gardener should 'enliven' the soil with special composts or manures. Their preparation was positively sacramental. Preparation 500, for example, involved stirring 45 grams of 'horn manure', made from cow dung, for an hour in about three gallons of lukewarm water. The container had to be free from all forms of contamination, the water was best taken from a spring, the stirring stick had to be chosen to 'suit personal convenience' and the stirring method was specific. 'Stir briskly until a deep crater is formed in the rotating liquid; then quickly reverse the direction of stirring and continue until the deep crater is formed once more.' The aim was to create a whirling liquid 'in a seething, chaotic turbulence', and the concoction had to be used within the hour, either sprayed on to the garden or flicked out of a bucket with a bunch of twigs. Soper's explanation for the benefits of this enlivening mixture proved a step too far for some vegetable-growers. 'Their main purpose is to stimulate and enhance the supersensible forces and influences working in from the far spaces of the cosmos and up from the centre of the earth.'

But the basics of biodynamics – helping to heal the earth, especially in the kitchen garden – proved to have a universal appeal. Now involved in related issues such as animal welfare, genetically modified food and sustainable farming, the international movement founded on Steiner's theories and Soper's interpretations shows no sign of running out of new recruits.

Husbandry at England's Great Houses

A century ago the idea of opening the kitchen garden to interested visitors would have seemed as odd as offering public tours of the coal cellar. The flower garden and shrubbery were the proper place for decorative delights, not the functional workplace that was the kitchen garden. Yet now gardens open to the public are inclined to include a kitchen garden in the tour; some, like Heligan and Audley End, have founded their reputations on their vegetable borders. Clearly people are genuinely interested in the plantings, the patterns and the structures of the vegetable plot.

While there is no economic imperative for people in America and northern Europe to grow their own fruit and vegetables (as there is during any downturn in the economy), waiting lists for allotments continue to grow in proportion to the scale of protests (even from non-gardeners) whenever plans are unveiled to redevelop them. Garden fashion has played its part in stimulating this vegetal interest, from the Arts and Crafts garden, where a trellis work of runner beans forms part of the romance, to William Robinson's and Gertrude Jekyll's popularising of the cottage garden with its intimate mix of flowers, fruit and vegetables.

Then there are the increasing number of crossover vegetables such as ruby chard, orach or even a plain pattern of lettuce, which add a frisson of interest to the increasingly informal flower border.

But perhaps there is a more basic attraction for this preoccupation with the fruits of the vegetable plot: people like to grow what they eat, and eat what they grow.

A glimpse into how a medieval kitchen garden might have looked is to be found at **Bayleaf**, an old, rescued farmhouse set in the grounds of the Weald and Downland Open Air Museum in West Sussex. The garden, recreated in front of the house, was designed with six plots of vegetables worked in a three-year rotation. Leeks, leaf beet and parsley are planted in the first year, coleworts or collards in the second, while in the third year the plots are manured during the winter then planted with onions the following spring. In summer all the plots come alive with colour as the undercrop of edible weeds, which are allowed to self seed each year, come into flower.

In the 1850s Queen Victoria made a handsome £50,000 from the sale of the old kitchen gardens at Kensington Palace, London. The money did not linger long in the royal coffers. The Queen and her husband Albert ploughed it back into a new kitchen garden at **Windsor**. Founded on the same principles as any other manor house kitchen garden of the time, it was built with a walled garden, hothouses and tools sheds. The scale of the enterprise, however, set it apart from the common lot.

One hundred and fifty gardeners worked within the 3.6-metre-high outer and inner walls that encircled the 27-acre garden – it was eventually expanded to 50 acres. In place of conventional gates, a porter's gatehouse led into the gardens. The head gardener lived on site in a house with a special suite of rooms where Albert and Victoria could enjoy a cream tea with fresh – very fresh – strawberries when they visited. There was an undergardener's house, too, built close to over 240 metres of hothouses. There were

Recreated in the medieval style, self-seeding edible weeds add a dash of colour to the vegetable plots at Bayleaf. (*Weald and Downland Open Air Museum*)

boiler rooms, potting sheds, mushroom houses, forcing pots, stables and, as a centrepiece for the garden, a fountain set in a 9-metre diameter basin.

The post-war fate that befell so many kitchen gardens would dispatch Victoria and Albert's kitchen garden too, leaving only its great walls behind. However, a century later another member of the royal family was planning a kitchen garden at his country house, **Highgrove** in Gloucestershire.

Prince Charles, the Prince of Wales, took advice from one of his neighbours, the garden author and lecturer Rosemary Verey.

Her Cotswold manor home garden at Barnsley House was a model of the twentieth-century English Arts and Crafts style with its mixed borders, formal *potager*, classical temple and modern knot. She had also established a decorative vegetable garden based on the designs of William Lawson's *Country Housewife's Garden* of the 1600s (and prompted a revival in the popularity of ruby chard). A new kitchen garden was constructed at Highgrove similarly laid out as a decorative *potager*. Appropriately enough, given the spirit of the new age, the vegetable garden was to be run on organic lines.

'Received from Mr Bryan £3 9s 4d for month's wages, also notice to leave at end of next month,' wrote William Cresswell in 1874. He was undergardener at **Audley End** near Saffron Walden in Essex. His diary, which petered out when he left Audley End, gave an insight into the life of the Victorian undergardener. William Cresswell had already contemplated leaving: 'Mr Bryan angry for not sending for him. Self troubled in mind with several things lately taken place in affair connected with situation, had thought of giving notice to leave.'

Twenty-two years old when he arrived from Cambridge to work at Audley End, William Cresswell lived in the bothy next to the great glasshouses (some of the oldest and largest in the UK), enjoying the benefits of central heating from the hot water pipes that ran through the bothy and into the greenhouses. Attached to the stately Jacobean manor house of Audley End, the walled vegetable garden, with over two miles of box hedging around the plots, fell into disuse in the Second World War, when house and grounds were passed into the hands of the state. Now restored by the Henry Doubleday Research Association, the UK's organic gardening association, and English Heritage, the gardens are open to the public and productive once again.

There are two Hampton Courts in England. The first, and more famous, is the Royal Palace near London, its gardens opened to the public by Queen Victoria in 1838. The second, in the rural West Midlands, features an imaginative decorative kitchen garden. It opened its gardens to the public in the 1990s.

Hampton Court in Herefordshire was founded in the early 1400s after the owner, Sir Roland Leinthall, 'toke many prisoners' at the battle of Agincourt, 'by which prey he beganne the new buildings of Hampton Court', according to one commentator. The manor followed the fortunes of many a rich manor house, one moment in favour and the subject of vast expenditure, at another in the doldrums, languishing in decay. The estate was purchased and sold by a succession of owners, including knights, a viscountess, a Member of Parliament and a petro-chemical multinational, before being rescued by a wealthy American couple.

In 1810 the estate, which had changed hands only once in the previous four centuries, was bought by Richard Arkwright, said to be 'the wealthiest commoner in England' after his father had made his fortune in the cotton industry. The upkeep of the estate was to drain the resources of three generations of the family over the next century. In the 1840s Joseph Paxton, architect of the Crystal Palace for the Great Exhibition in London, designed a new conservatory. At the close of the century owner Johnny Arkwright patented a successful design for a wooden box made to carry vegetables and fruit without damaging the contents. It was not enough to restore the wealth of the Arkwrights, who sold up in 1911. The house changed hands six more times before Americans Robert and Judith Van Kampens bid unsuccessfully for the estate at auction. Nevertheless they visited the house out of curiosity in 1994, met the vendors and within ten minutes had agreed a sale.

The Van Kampens spent $17.5 million on the restoration of the house and gardens. The Van Kampens gardens, designed by artist and

The kitchen gardens at the 500-year-old Hampton Court estate were restored by an American millionaire. (*Photo: Sabina Ruber/Hampton Court Estate*)

gardener, Simon Dorrell, have been described as one of the most ambitious garden creations of the 1990s. The design included a maze of a thousand yews with a gothic tower at its centre. Below the tower an underground tunnel led to a waterfall and a sunken garden. But key to the design were the flowers and decorative vegetables laid out within the original Victorian garden walls and divided up by canals, a pair of octagonal pavilions and pleached avenues. Organic produce from the kitchen garden was used to supply a restaurant housed in Paxton's now restored greenhouse. When Robert Van Kampens died in 1999, Hampton Court remained open to the public as a new buyer was sought for this extraordinary vegetable garden.

In 1772 the kitchen garden at **Clumber Park** near Worksop in Nottinghamshire supplied fresh vegetables and fruit to the 100-strong household of the Dukes of Newcastle. Garden walls enclosed around four acres of land, but there was another six acres of ground under fruit and vegetable cultivation. It included an acre of glass housing, forcing sheds and mushroom houses. Close by a pair of ice houses were used to store fresh produce. Even in the early

The old kitchen garden at Clumber Park, photographed here around 1935, has been restored and is now run on organic lines. (*National Trust, East Midlands*)

1900s the gardens required twenty-nine fulltime gardeners to grow and harvest crops from everyday carrots and potatoes to exotics such as chillies, sweet corn, pineapple and sugar cane.

In 1938 the manor house was destroyed, but remarkably the vegetable gardens had been saved for the nation by the National Trust. By the 1990s a tiny team of three fulltime gardeners and a group of volunteers managed the old kitchen garden and its 137-metre-long glasshouse, raising organic vegetable crops as they would have been grown in the late eighteenth century.

What was to become one of the most famous vegetable gardens of the twentieth century started life as a kitchen garden in the late 1700s. Henry Hawkins Tremayne had been curate of Loswithiel in Cornwall when he unexpectedly inherited an estate. It was called The Willows, but went by the Cornish name for willow, **Heligan**. The family estate, which stretched from Gorran to Mevagissey, was spread across over 100 acres of south-west Cornwall. It was large enough to encompass several farms, its own flour mill, brickworks, sawmill, brewery and a kitchen garden of nearly two acres. Produce from the garden helped to feed not only the family and their guests, but also the twenty inside staff and up to twenty-two outside staff. Henry Tremayne busied himself with Heligan, laying out the gardens more or less as they appear today. Three further generations carried the horticultural work forward until June 1914, when two shots from an assassin's pistol in faraway Sarajevo sounded what was to be the opening salvo of the First World War. It is doubtful whether Heligan's water boy or flowerpot cleaner knew any-thing about the incident, but already the political repercussions were rippling across Europe. By August of that year they were lapping up against the walls of the big house.

'Don't come here to sleep or slumber,' scribbled one of the gardeners on the lavatory wall as each of his mates signed his name

Beaver tail glass panes on the restored glasshouses at Heligan ensured that rainwater drained from the middle of the glass, thus protecting the side timbers.

and added the date: August 1914. By the time of the hollow victory of Armistice Day in 1918, three in every ten males who had been aged between 24 and 13 at the outbreak of war were dead. They included half the staff of Heligan. Heligan, like so many other grand houses, went into a post-war decline.

That was until one winter's day in 1999 when entrepreneurs Tim Smit and John Nelson went exploring and stumbled upon what Smit would later describe as the horticultural equivalent of the Marie Celeste. 'John and I stumbled across a tiny room buried under fallen masonry in a heavy shrouded corner of the walled garden. Here we found those barely legible signatures in its faded, lime-washed walls.'

Ambitiously they decided to restore Heligan. Early efforts were concentrated on the glasshouse fruits and the famous pineapple pit, but it was the 1.8-acre vegetable garden that became what Tim Smit called the engine room of the house. Whole trees and brambles four metres high were cleared from the plot. After ploughing and laying the water pipes, the classic cruciform of paths was relaid and, under the shade of fruit hoops, the four quarters of the vegetable garden were restored.

The Heligan gardeners, fixing a benchmark of the mid-1800s, set out to recreate the Victorian vegetable garden, selecting plants on the basis of taste and flavour and growing them without either the supposed benefits of modern pesticides, herbicides or fertilisers or the conventional garden poisons of the Victorian age such as nicotine, arsenic and red lead. Eventually Heligan was supplying its own restaurant and, with a vegetable box scheme, the local neighbourhood with produce from the kitchen garden.

Villandry: The World's Most Decorative Vegetable Garden

The château at **Villandry** is one of a rash of country houses that lines the Loire valley in France. When a Dr Joachim Carvallo took over the restoration of its formal gardens in the early 1900s, aided on the expenses side by his marriage to a wealthy American heiress, he created one of the world's most decorative vegetable gardens.

Dr Carvallo restored Villandry's eighteenth-century gardens, designed to be viewed from the high windows of the château basing his work on the engravings of French manor gardens from the 1600s by Jacques Androuet du Cerceau.

There was the *Jardin d'Ornement* designed by a Spanish artist Lozano to symbolise four stages of love, its box hedges enclosing plants to suggest hearts, flames, masks, fans and dagger blades (for *l'amour tragique*). Then there was the *Jardin d'Eau*, an ornamental basin connected to a canal and filled with carp. But the glory of the garden was the *Jardin Potager*, a feature that still attracts visitors from around the world.

Separated from the *Jardin d'Ornement* by an avenue of limes, the *Jardin Potager* was constructed of nine square quarters, each with its

Ornamental vegetables decorate the gardens at Villandry in France's Loire valley.

own geometric parterre and hedged with low-growing box. Carvallo filled his parterres, not with lavish blooms, stately shrubs, or coloured stones, as some did, but with everyday French vegetables – over 30,000 of them. Packed together in a mazelike design, there were ruby chard and tomatoes, decorative cabbage and carrots, basil, aubergines and black pimiento. Dr Joachim Carvallo had created the world's most spectacular ornamental potager.

4

Tools, Potting and Pests

The Kitchen Gardener

Children raised on the writings of Beatrix Potter will remember the guardian of the garden in *The Tale of Peter Rabbit*. 'Your father had an accident there; he was put in a pie by Mrs McGregor,' warns Peter Rabbit's mother at the start of the story. The young rabbit ate 'lettuces, and some French beans, and then he ate some radishes; and then, feeling rather sick, he went to look for some parsley'. At this point he came face to face with the curmudgeonly Mr McGregor. The bearded Mr McGregor endeavoured to stamp Peter Rabbit to death.

In the post-war years of the Second World War an equally sanguine figure featured in an instructional cartoon column in the *Sunday Express*. This was Adam the Gardener, who, like Mr McGregor, had about him an almost detectable smell of stale pipe smoke, charity shop clothes and underwear that received irregular washing. Both vegetable-growers, Adam and Mr McGregor, had, as their antecedents, the garden staff of Edwardian England, those churlish servants who would do only what they would do. How did this stereotype arise? And what became of him?

The *hortolanus* or *gardinarius* was a person of status in medieval Europe. The *hortolanus* administered the monastery gardens, overseeing the workers who tilled the soil, planted the garlic and the beans, grafted the fruit stock and ensured that the cloister garden remained free of moss and weeds. The workers were often lay gardeners, for, although the early Benedictines and Cistercians exhorted their brethren to till the soil themselves, believing that hard work and abstinence brought one closer to God, they were also very good at recruiting novices from the nobility. The noble brother, however devout, preferred to pay a lay person to do his digging for him. Outside the monastery walls,

Digging deep, a seventeenth-century gardener trenches the soil in the vegetable garden. (*John Loudon, Encyclopaedia of Gardening*)

meanwhile, people looked after their vegetable plots as and when they could in the evenings and, as religious rules permitted, at weekends.

In the 1500s, as the prosperity of the Elizabethan age edged across Britain from the south-east to the north and west, Britons spent their newfound money, as they always will, on smart homes and fine gardens in what the landscape historian W.G. Hoskins described as the Great Rebuilding of Britain. We can only assume that women were the mistresses of these gardens: as William Fitzherbert noted in his 1538 *The Book of Husbandrie*: 'the beginning of March . . . is time for a wife to make her garden.' Although evidence of the woman's role as the kitchen gardener goes largely unrecorded (apart from occasional accounts of women paid as weeding labourers), common sense suggests that the housewife who managed the household would have kept a close eye on the productive vegetable garden. Early garden authors such as Thomas Tusser – they were all men – suggest that women's work was confined to the flowers, herbs and medicinal plants. However, in 1617 William Lawson was completing his *Countrie Housewifes Garden*, offering advice on the kitchen garden, 'Planting, Graffing, and to make Ground good for a rich Orchard' and on the 'Husbandry of Bees, with their several Uses and Annoyances'. Charles Evelyn, son of the garden writer and designer John Evelyn, published *The Lady's Recreation* in 1717.

In the early 1800s women gardeners were gaining a higher profile. When Jane Webb, the daughter of a Birmingham engineer, married the prolific garden writer John Loudon, she helped her husband with his books and encyclopaedia and wrote a series of books for women gardeners including *Gardening for Ladies* and *The Ladies' Flower-Garden*. She also edited *The Ladies' Companion*, which was founded in 1849. Loudon, twenty-four years her senior, made little concession to the role of the women in the kitchen garden. A labourer's garden, he wrote, for example, should be large enough to occupy the man in digging and planting and those of 'the female part of the family' or the 'wife and children in hoeing, weeding and watering'. It echoed the attitude of the times epitomised by the King of Sweden's alleged aside to his wife: 'Madam, I married you to give me children, not to give me advice.'

Times were changing. In 1913 suffragettes attacked the clubby men's world of the garden in their campaign for votes for women. 'Mad women raid Kew' ran one newspaper headline after women protesters broke in and destroyed plants in the orchid house at the Royal Botanic Gardens. Fifteen years earlier the heiress Ellen Willmott (who died penniless after spending her fortune on her gardens) was awarded the coveted Victorian Medal of Honour for her horticultural work. She shared it with 'the rather fat, and rather grumbly' Gertrude Jekyll, who herself managed a substantial kitchen garden at her home in Munstead Wood, Surrey. The description of Miss Jekyll came from another woman gardener who would become one of the most influential voices in gardening, Vita Sackville-West.

However, although Gertrude Jekyll and Ellen Willmott both had a reputation for hands-on gardening, their most useful gardening tool was the jobbing gardener himself (Ellen Willmott employed over a hundred gardeners at her Warley Place garden in Essex). For two millennia at least, jobbing gardeners in the kitchen garden were the ones 'grubbing weeds from gravel paths', as Rudyard Kipling put it in his poem 'The Glory of the Garden' in 1911. Cheap, and good at all those back-breaking jobs such as manuring, digging and weeding the vegetable plot, the jobbing gardener was also the ideal tool for planting out and protecting tender seedlings, and harvesting and storing crops.

Low wages and perpetual servitude were the constant lot of the jobbing gardener. But job satisfaction featured too.

Jobbing gardeners, like lighthouse-keepers and clergymen, were a curious and sometimes eccentric breed. They were too isolated by their livelihood to have formed a trade-union movement, and their pay traditionally hovered around the agricultural wage. They were often illiterate: Richard Payne Knight, the scholar who made a name for himself when he attacked Capability Brown's landscape style, ran his estate at Downton, Herefordshire, with the aid of gardener who 'is an extremely simple laborer. He does not know a letter or a figure.'

If things went wrong in the garden, the jobbing gardener could, and often did, take the blame: 'If those who have private gardens were a little more difficult to please in selecting a gardener, and in the quality of the produce sent to table, the consequences would be an improvement in that produce, and more scientific gardeners,' insisted Loudon.

However, while most paid gardeners had to be content with their servitude, some, especially in Victorian and Edwardian times, rose through the social ranks to become men of status and influence. When the bachelor gardener William Robinson died in 1935, he left a 360-acre estate, including an acre of kitchen garden, and the Elizabethan manor house of Gravetye in Sussex. He was the wealthiest garden writer of his time, yet he had begun his working life as the garden boy at Curraghmore in Ireland. By 21 he had risen to the rank of foreman in charge of the precious glasshouses on an estate in County Laois. Said to have abandoned his hothouse charges in the middle of the night, the windows open and the fires extinguished, after an argument with the owner, Robinson had set off to Dublin to find a new post. It was a good story, if an unlikely one, for he soon found a job with the Royal Botanic Society in London's Regents Park and began contributing articles to the *Gardener's Chronicle*. *The Times* sent him to Paris as their horticultural correspondent and by 1868 he had published his first book, *Gleanings from French Gardens*. The once-poor, apprentice gardener never looked back. He set up a magazine, the *Garden*, in 1875, recruiting that other influential writer, Gertrude Jekyll, who would herself edit the magazine at the century's turn in 1899. The *Garden* was sold and merged with *House and Gardens* in 1927, but Robinson had already founded another magazine, *Gardening Illustrated*, aimed at the up-and-coming suburban and villa gardeners. By 1838 this gardener turned publisher was employing his own army of gardeners when he bought Gravetye Manor. His relations with his gardening staff and head gardener Ernest Markham were said to be good. (When he died, his last wish, to be cremated, was fulfilled: he had been an early campaigner for cremation.)

In Robinson's day the gardener's craft was handed down from generation to generation. When the late George Watkins, a former head gardener on a Shropshire estate, started work in the early 1900s, his education was a hand-me-down affair: 'I worked under a very clever gardener, George Crew. He had a wonderful way of teaching. He'd give me some packets of seed then he'd keep an eye on me, like, and I got to grow those seeds on, potting on and that sort of thing. With this coaching, he never did anything without he told me what he was doing and the why and the wherefore.'

As a boy the gardener-to-be would join the house staff as pot washer and apprentice, spending a year or so in the kitchen garden on menial tasks, before moving to spend another year or two on the flower borders. An ambitious young gardener might move on to be a journeyman, settling at another garden for a period. In this way he would improve his skills and widen his knowledge until he could apply for his first post as foreman at a large garden or head gardener at a smaller establishment.

In an era when it was fashionable to keep a fine garden, but unfashionable to get the earth beneath one's nails, the position of head gardener was a potentially prestigious one. But for most who maintained the nation's gardens and grew the household's vegetables, their social ranking 'below stairs' was relatively low. 'You had to touch your cap to all these toffs, you see,' recalls George Watkins. The post had its advantages. Watkins recalls: 'When I was a boy starting in the gardens, gardeners worked until four o'clock on a Saturday, but farmers till five or six. In 1920, 1921, when I was in Yorkshire, I didn't have to work after twelve o'clock on a Saturday. That was strange to me.' When he moved to Shropshire his Saturday afternoons remained garden-free because the local squire for whom he worked had a passion for village cricket. 'Sir Henry Ripley, he'd got a great Daimler tourer that could take the whole team: that was how keen he was on the village team.'

Generally, however, social class dictated that the gardener and his lordship were not seen in society together. While the gardener might carry on undisturbed in the vegetable plot, he was expected to keep a low profile in the rest of the garden and remove himself if there were guests about. The kitchen gardener was a necessary nuisance. The mistress of the house had to produce a good table of vegetables and the key to production was her kitchen garden staff: friction between the mistress of the house and the kitchen gardener could have serious consequences. In fiction, P.G. Wodehouse's Lord Emsworth was continually frustrated by his sister's head gardener, McAllister. Fact is stranger than fiction: the stubborn jobbing gardener on one large estate in the English Midlands regularly received a tray of young lettuce seedlings from his mistress for planting out. Just as regularly, the gardener made sure they caught a late frost or were taken by slugs, while informing his mistress that her plants had failed once again because the local ground was just not good enough for them.

One commentator in the 1800s, John Latouche, condemned such relationships: 'Have you no spirit left that you submit to be dictated to by a servant?' he asked. Occasionally the owner made her displeasure public. Baroness Rolle of Bicton in Devon did so of her head gardener, James Barnes, in the 1860s, telling friends that, when he left her service, he had abandoned Bicton in a disordered state. Barnes sued the Honourable Baroness for libel, winning the case in 1869 and receiving the equivalent of two years' pay, £200, in compensation.

It seems that the grim Mr McGregor, the dour Adam and the intractable McAllister owe their reputations to these stern Edwardian and Victorian gardeners.

Spade, Hoe and Hook

Not normally a day of special celebration, 1 September is, nevertheless, the feast day of the patron saint of the spade, St Fiacre. In the 600s Fiacre left his native Ireland for France, where he was welcomed by the Burgundian-born Bishop Faro of Meaux. Faro gave Fiacre a piece of land to found a monastery near what is now Saint-Fiacre-en-Brie. But he imposed one troublesome condition: the monastery could occupy only so much land as could be dug by one man in one day.

Fiacre himself took up the challenge with his trusty spade. When the sun set Fiacre had turned the sod of no less than nine acres. A hermitage was founded on the site and hermitage it was: women were strictly excluded and, even after Fiacre's death, any that trespassed were said to suffer mysterious misfortunes.

Fiacre was destined for sainthood. His reputation as a gardener and a grower of fine vegetables was eclipsed only by his phenomenal powers for curing haemorrhoids. His chapel and shrine are at Meaux and his emblem is, of course, the spade. (His memory was also enshrined by Parisian cab drivers. When the four-wheeled cabs first appeared for hire in the French capital close by the Hôtel Saint-Fiacre, they were known as *fiacres*.)

Irish links with the spade have continued down the ages. Gangs of Irish 'inland navigators' or navvies formed the backbone of the men who built Britain's railways and canals. They worked with the same basic hand tool as St Fiacre, although it was hand-crafted to their own designs. A century ago the craft had developed into one of local distinctiveness, as the men of the Ulster spade mills made different spades to meet the specific demands of local soils and local traditions. They manufactured more than 100 different types from the thin, bladed 'loys' of the south and west of Ireland to the dependable two-shouldered Ulster digging spade. There were mud

A choice selection of garden tools marketed by Sutton's Seeds in the 1890s. (*Suttons Consumer Products Ltd*)

spades and drain spades, trench spades and *slanes* for cutting peat. Each was fitted with an ash handle, and designs even took account of the fact that the Irish gardener traditionally dug the kitchen garden with his right foot, but the Englishman with his left.

The forerunner of the spade was a very down-to-earth implement, the mattock or, in Ireland, the *matóg*. The mattock was spade, hoe, trencher and root-digger. A close relative of the adze, the housebuilder's axe used to fashion green and unseasoned oak into housebeams, and the butcher's pole axe, the mattock had a broad blade at the one end and a blunt point at the other. As metal technology improved, the garden fork, hand trowel, four-pronged fork and hoe tended to push the mattock to the back of the tool shed (although it still serves rural communities across the globe).

Weeding might be done with a hoe or a forked stick and a hook 'ground sharpe both behind and before', as suggested by William Fitzherbert in *The Book of Husbandrie*, while the thorny problem of clearing virgin ground was solved with a hook or bill hook. The design of the hook, like that of any other tool prior to the Industrial Revolution, varied from region to region, even from parish to parish. In England alone more than twenty-five designs have been recorded for hedge making, pruning and cutting back and harvesting stakes and poles from the woods: 'by hook and by crook' was the legal term for working the manor woods.

The bill hook's smaller brother, the sickle, was a harvesting tool, handy for topping large quantities of carrot or beet before they were put to store in sand or peat, and for clearing paths and around fruit trees. Down the years a favourite sickle would come to resemble the cusp of a new moon with its thin, razor-edged blade. The bill hook's big brother, the scythe, came into its own in the autumn for mowing the long meadow or orchard grass. In times of trouble and political unrest, such as the 1381 Peasants' Revolt, all four – mattock, scythe, sickle and hook – were appropriated from the tool store and born as lethal weapons for close combat fighting. (History would repeat itself when the garden tool shed was once again raided in the Second World War by weaponless Home Guardsmen.)

A basic tool set illustrated by John Evelyn in the 1660s shows a conventional range of tools, including wooden sieves for sifting potting soil, seed sowing boxes, dibbers and wooden rakes lined with timber teeth. Those 'wedge(d) with oke' were the superior sort. If Evelyn were to journey forward in time for three and a half centuries, he might be amused to find the hoe, rake, hook and shears of his age still in use (but he would be confounded by the quantity of plastics used in the garden).

The start of Queen Victoria's reign marked the start of mass marketing in the kitchen garden tool trade. During her 64-year tenure – she died in 1901 – she ruled a quarter of the globe and one in four of every person on it. Her servants gardened in far-flung corners of the empire: 'Your Le Floral is the most remarkable stuff,' wrote Sergeant-Major J. Binns of Pachmarhi, Central Provinces, East India, to Sutton & Sons ('seedsmen to His Imperial Majesty the German Emperor') in 1837, a company that, in common with the garden tool makers, offered 'carriage paid to all the principal ports in England when orders amount to 60s'.

Victoria's long reign would witness the transformation of the kitchen garden and the tools that turned it. In 1851 her husband, Prince Albert, organised the Great Exhibition at the Crystal Palace in London. More than 100,000 exhibits were displayed, including the very latest in kitchen-garden technology. One gardener who attended the Great Exhibition, but then refused to go inside because he disapproved of the 'ugly' exhibits, was the 18-year-old William Morris. He thought the Exhibition had been hijacked by the nation's industrialists and used as a vehicle to promote mass production. (Morris's Arts and Crafts movement would one day spread to garden design, espousing the cause of the Romantic medieval garden and its handsome hand tools.)

Six million attended the Exhibition and they had money to spend. Their tool stores were soon filled with every conceivable horticultural device. Sutton's, for example, could offer a choice of three dozen garden penknives including a special asparagus knife, a ladies budding knife, a pruning knife and saw ('superior') and a knife with two blades and botanical lens; there were seven different spades and twenty-two different hoes; five 'Improved Garden Engines' (or wheeled water barrels) and eight wheelbarrows with a choice of wooden or iron wheels; and no less than twenty-eight different carts for carrying manure.

Two world wars later, and with no labour force to use the tools, the tool sheds were full of dusty relics. Some were profitably tidied away with the latest American invention, the shadowboard, which offered a proper place for every tool. Most, however, were thrown on the scrap heap, as steel and plastic usurped the old iron and ash, or hickory-handled tools. In the post-war period new tools for the kitchen garden were designed to help the single-handed owner gardener to manage on his or her own. The ubiquitous mechanical tiller, which took America by storm, was invented by a Swiss gardener, based on his observations of a dog digging for a bone.

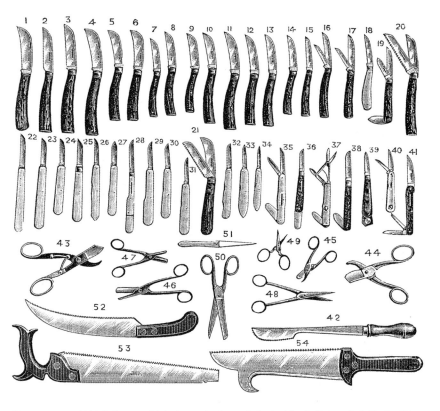

There was a special blade for every job in the garden from a ladies budding knife to a slip knife, for slicing off a suitable cutting. (*Suttons Consumer Products Ltd*)

Meanwhile, wheeled hoes and powered ploughs, steel wheelbarrows and chainsaws, strimmers and chuntering motor mowers flooded the market – Sunday mornings would never be quiet again.

Innovations included hopeless failures like the hand weeding glove of 1965, which dripped with weedkiller and was used to stroke offending weeds to death, and spectacular successes like the Flymo for gliding over grassy paths between the vegetable beds and the

Style icon. The Opinel, first created by Jo Opinel in 1890, came in twelve different sizes.

Gro-bag, which allowed people with no garden to grow a small crop of vegetables.

Nevertheless certain kitchen garden hand tools did stand the test of time. They included the hand trowel, the French secateurs, introduced by the garden writer William Robinson and, in France at least, the Opinel penknife. Jo Opinel lived in the Savoy region of France and created his Swiss army knife of the kitchen garden in 1890. With its hardened steel blade held in place by a steel ring and its palm-shaped wooden handle, the Opinel came in twelve different sizes, each carrying the trade mark symbol of a crowned hand. (The Opinel owner was expected to drill a hole in the handle himself and run a cord through so that it could hang from his trouser belt.) While Pablo Picasso was said to have used his favourite Opinel to carve small sculptures, one alpinist owed his own life to his trusty Opinel: buried in an avalanche in 1959, Pierre Paquet used his Opinel to cut a way out of his snow tomb. But for the most part the Opinel served the French kitchen gardeners for a century of slicing onions, trimming bean sticks and cutting raffia. William Morris would have approved.

How Big Is my Garden?

Measurement is an essential tool in the vegetable garden. It always was. Early Frankish law dictated that, for the purposes of legal compensation, an orchard had to consist of at least twelve trees in an enclosure 60 feet by 80 feet. 'The Brazil beet requires eighteen inches; and the plants a foot and a half asunder for the crop sown in April,' declared the garden writer Shirley Hibberd in the late 1800s. 'Cabbage. Sow thinly 1 inch deep. As soon as the plants have made four or five leaves they should be planted out from 24 inches apart,' advised one post-war garden guide.

The desire for accuracy in the vegetable beds can become an obsession. With her husband away fighting, this Second World War West Midlands housewife was determined to dig for victory to supplement her rations. 'I dug up the front lawn and learned to grow vegetables from my neighbour. He was an old man and he always used a tape measure not only between the rows but between the plants too.' This veteran gardener relied on the imperial system, in use in Britain for 600 years until the British Parliament voted to go metric in 1963.

The principal unit of measurement has always been the human body – horses are still measured in hands, people still pace out their plots and sow with a pinch of seeds. A foot, a step and an arm span were useful measures in the Middle Ages when Henry I legalised his 'imperial' measure of the foot and the yard (three feet), which was based on the distance between the tip of the Royal nose and the thumb of his outstretched arm. Before he died in 1135, an Iron Yard of Our Lord King was lodged in London and exact copies, cast in bronze or brass, were delivered throughout the kingdom.

Five thousand years ago the boundaries surrounding the farms and vegetable gardens along the River Nile were regularly washed away and the Egyptians used a rope of 100 cubits, the cubits marked by knots, to re-establish the garden boundaries. The Royal Cubit was cast from a block of black granite against which every cubit measuring stick was checked for accuracy. The cubit could be subdivided into twenty-eight 'digits' and the construction of the pyramids demonstrates the success of their system.

Two thousand two hundred years ago the first Emperor of China, Shih Hung Tio, fixed a standard measure of length, a *chih*. It was 250mm long and based on the distance between the pulse and the base of the thumb. The *chang* was approximately 3 metres long.

When the centre of power in the Middle East swung away from Egypt towards the Mediterranean, it was the turn of the Greeks, who, still using a variant on the finger, adapted the Egyptian cubit to equal 24 fingers. They made their basic unit of length one foot or 16 fingers. When it was the Roman's turn to set a worldwide standard, they too used the foot, but subdivided it into *uncia* or twelfths. Longer lengths were measured as a pace, which was two steps, one with the left foot, one with the right and a thousand paces made a *mille*, or a mile.

A foot, a step or an arm span were still useful garden measures in the Middle Ages. While merchants measured their wool in *ells*, the distance between the elbow and the fingertip, and the Vikings measured a fathom as so many lengths of a sailor's arm, the medieval vegetable garden was measured in feet. A standard size, measured with an 84-foot cord on a triangulation of 3: 4: 5 (21 feet,

28 feet and 35 feet) produced a vegetable plot 28 foot long and 21 foot wide. The plot could be divided into four or five strips, narrow enough to allow the bed to be cultivated without the gardener walking across it and compacting the soil. 'Beds should be so contrived that the hands of those who weed them may easily reach the middle of their breadth, so that those who are weeding may not be forced to tread on seedlings, to the help of which let the paths be of such a width (as a man's foot) that they may weed first one half and then the other half of the bed,' advised Thomas Hill very sensibly in 1577.

Larger garden areas occurred in the village 'clos' (in Scandinavian the 'toft'), a strip of ground at the rear of the cottage, measuring between 30 and 60 feet wide and between 200 and 600 feet long. Although part of the patch would be put down to pasture and orchard and part devoted to that wonder material of the medieval age, flax or hemp, a significant area would be dug by foot ready for planting the worts. The furlong, an eighth of a mile and based on the distance a horse could plough without needing to pause for a rest, was more of an agricultural measure, but the acre, representing a patch of ground that a team of oxen could plough in a day, was, and still is, used for larger gardens. The acre measured 4,840 square yards and could be subdivided into 160 perches, from the Latin pole or staff. Measuring the feet of the first sixteen parishioners leaving the church on a Sunday was judged a sound method of establishing a perch.

Apart from the addition of the 22-yard-long 'chain' introduced by Edmund Gunter, the astronomer and mathematician whose surveyor's chain was used to measure America, the imperial system served the vegetable gardeners of England unchallenged until 1791.

Then in post-revolutionary France, a committee of the French Academy of Science defined a new, revolutionary unit of measurement, the metre, so-called after the Greek word *metron* or

Even the French proved reluctant to measure their gardens by the 'new' metric measure. A dozen brassicas dictated the ideal width of a potager.

measure. The committee of twelve based the system on multiples of ten and the basic unit, the metre, on one ten-millionth of the distance between the Equator and the North Pole. Unable actually to measure that distance, two French engineers calculated it after measuring the more manageable distance between Dunkirk and Barcelona.

When the new metric system was adopted, the Gallic equivalent of the Egyptian's granite cubit was made of platinum iridium and stored at Sèvres. Plaques showing the standard measure were put up in public places across France. The metric system was introduced to the USA over a century ago, but largely ignored by gardeners. And after forty years of the metric system in British gardens, there is a marked reluctance amongst gardeners to use anything other than King Henry's imperial standard. Despite the advent of the motor car, the aeroplane and the computer, allotment dimensions continued to be based on the measurements of the Middle Ages: section 22 of the Allotments Act 1922 describes an allotment garden as 'not exceeding forty poles in extent'.

Under Glass

In some parts of the Dutch Lowlands the sight of naked soil is a rarity. Instead a sea of glass covers the polders and protects acres of vegetables ripening with all the advantages of free solar power. Now, in the new, mechanised age of gardening, the Dutch glasshouses hum with the computers that control the hydroponically grown tomatoes and cucumber plants. Not for nothing were glass-covered vegetable frames, or Dutch lights, so named.

Just under four centuries ago, John Evelyn explained his own method of harnessing natural energy to grow plants when he delivered his Philosphical Discourse on Earth to the Royal Society, an organisation established by Charles II and devoted to promoting the arts and sciences. Evelyn explained how forcing pits, deep enough for a man to stand in, could be filled with steaming dung. Plants grown on portable wooden trays over the pits positively thrived with this natural bottom heat.

Shirley Hibberd in his *Profitable Gardening* gave the forcing pit his vote: 'In times gone by there was nothing better than the hothouse frame or pit, heated with leaves and stable manure, and in skilful hands there was generally no difficulty in obtaining plenty of fruit.' But, he warned, 'the dung-frame was very uncertain of productiveness'.

Evelyn and his Discourse helped to promote the 'greenhouse' and the 'conservatory', both places where gardeners could conserve their green plants over winter. Early experimenters used wood, stone and brick to create greenhouses, but by 1697 the Duke of Devonshire had one of the first glass greenhouses built at Chatsworth. By then designers knew that ventilation was vital, that the reflective quality of whitewashed walls raised the temperature inside, and that a glass roof set at a slope of precisely 52 degrees would maximise the effects of the sun, which, at midday, struck the glass at right angles.

Technical developments were spurred on by a mania for growing tender plants especially the pine or pineapple, by the repeal of a tax on glass in the 1840s and by nations competing to build the most spectacular winter gardens. The 90-metre-long Jardin d'Hiver in Paris's Champs Elysées rose up almost three stories high in 1847, while a vine house at Buffalo in the USA housed over 200 vines in its 210 metre length. However, the greenhouse and the conservatory went in opposite directions, especially after Joseph Paxton built his prestigious Crystal Palace in 1851: the conservatory became an aspirational addition to the Victorian villa, while the greenhouse was turned into an essential tool to service the Victorian table.

Shirley Hibberd regarded the greenhouse as a thing of beauty. 'A houseful of melons or cucumbers, showing a rich screen of foliage between the eye and the sun, and the fruits hanging below it, as they would naturally if the plants were twining among the trees of their native soils, is one of the finest sights in the whole range of horticultural exhibitions.'

Technical advances in glass making powered the development of the greenhouse. In the early 1800s broad or cylinder glass was blown into a cylinder and then opened out flat to be cut into sheets. Plate glass, where molten glass was poured out onto a casting table and then laboriously ground and polished smooth, was introduced in the late 1800s. Both were too expensive for horticultural use. The alternative was crown glass, which was spun into a large disc and then cut into squares and diamonds, the bull's eye centre being thrown back into the furnace. John Loudon declared that 'economy, as to the quality of glass' was self-defeating and would result in 'the sickly pale etiolated appearance of plants more painful than agreeable to the eye of any who take an interest in the vegetable kingdom'. When Sir Joseph Paxton designed a cast iron glazing bar with a rain water channel on the upper side and a condensation channel on the inner face (freely taken from nature – the Paxton gutter was modelled on the leaf of a giant water lily), it opened the floodgates on a frenzy of greenhouse building. There were great, double span cucumber houses and meloneries, modest plant preservers, 'lawn' conservatories 'invaluable for the use of Amateurs in the forwarding of . . . various seeds', pit frames, lean-to greenhouses and lean-to forcing houses calculated to 'convince all practical minds of the importance and utility of this class of House for Gentlemen, Nurserymen, Market Gardeners, and, in fact, all those who require a cheap, strong House for Forcing, or growing Cucumbers, Tomatoes, Melons, &c, &c'.

Outside the glasshouse gardeners rich and poor took advantage of the cold frame and the French cloche, originally a bell-shaped glass (hence its name), to bring on early vegetables or shelter late ones from the autumn frosts. Inside the greenhouse a variety of heating systems were tried out from pits of tan bark (sheets of oak used in the tanning industry), which reached temperatures up to 42°C, to anthracite, charcoal or coke stoves. There were devices for waking the undergardener in the middle of the night should the temperature fall too low, but fire alarms were less well developed and glasshouses frequently burned down.

As early as the 1750s early vegetables were being produced by running cast iron pipes filled with heated water beneath the beds. The concept is at least 1,000 years old, according to Ibn Bassāl,

Old and new, the great glasshouse at Kew, built by Decimus Burton and Richard Turner, and its twentieth-century contemporary, a domestic greenhouse for tomatoes.

gardener to the Sultan of Toledo, who wrote a book in the 1000s discussing water supply, soil and its preparation. He gave detailed instruction on raising early seedlings. A dung heap of slightly dried mule dung, pepped up with a soupçon of pigeon dung, was built first. Seeds were then sown on top in a compost of dry dung and sheltered with cabbage leaves. The natural bottom heat helped the seeds germinate and grow. The heap could maintain its heat for up to five weeks, but it could prove unreliable: if the heap overheated it would cook, rather than cultivate, the young plants.

Eventually the safer system of steam pipes, laid like a conventional central system, took over in the great glasshouses, while today many gardeners germinate their seed using a little 'bottom heat' in the form of an electric cable.

Like the walled gardens that sheltered them, the great glasshouses eventually slipped into decline, as the cost of fuel and labour made them uneconomical. But in the country homes of the 1920s the greenhouse still had a role to play, as Shropshire head gardener George Watkins remembered:

Between the front of the house and the servant's quarters at the back, you had the old green baize door. There's a bell there to ring madam. You'd go in about ten o'clock in the morning to meet the lady in the kitchen and discuss what vegetables she'd like. You got to try and get about three vegetables a day and you couldn't put the same three vegetables in on the run so you got to get so many varieties to follow on all the year round.

There was a big conservatory and a heated greenhouse. Heating was so cheap in those days a truck-load of anthracite would be enough to keep you going for the winter. In the conservatory side was vines, then you got to grow carnations, 'chrysanths', cinerarias and cyclamen for the lady. Off that again you'd got a plant house where you forced potatoes and beans and tomatoes and cucumbers and anything like that. We used to force dwarf beans, salsify, carrots, beetroots and celeriac – you name it, we got it.

The Potting Shed

The potting shed (originally a sloping roof or penthouse to shed off the rain, offers the *New Gresham English Dictionary*) was an essential item in the vegetable garden. Home to an assortment of broken tools waiting (in vain) to be mended, cropping plans and seed catalogues, old kitchen scales for weighing prize vegetables and a patched-up chair or two, the potting shed was also a wet weather sanctuary. It was largely an invention of the gardening boom of the Victorian age.

Until the Middle Ages the division between the ornamental garden and the kitchen garden was vague. Although monasteries created clear boundaries between the cloister garden, cellarer's garden and orchard, the yeoman's wife who lived nearby would be content to mix a rose or two among her coleworts and peas. (The damask rose, brought back to England by returning Crusaders, was a useful 'first-aid' flower, regularly used to treat coughs, colds, eye infections and, according to John Gerard, 'staunch bleedings'). As garden fashions developed, however, the kitchen garden of the 1700s and 1800s was banished to the back of the house, away from the fine flower borders and hand-clipped lawns.

Out of sight was not out of mind, however, and enthusiastic amateurs like the Revd Gilbert White would certainly have shepherded guests around his vegetable patch so that they might share his pride in the 'four rows of marrow-fat pease' or his concerns with the vagaries of the weather: 'Sowed a crop of carrots, parsneps, beets, radishes, lettuce, Leeks, Onions; a small crop of Salsafy; red

Cabbage-seed, Dutch parsley & Chardoons. There had been a glut of wet for five weeks, & the Ground was rather too moist; but worked pretty well.'

A century later quiet pride is evident in the letters of vegetable-growers to the seed companies. One gardener declared his Dean's Early Prolific cucumber 'perfect in form and very solid' and Mr William Morton of Shepton Mallet felt compelled to put pen to paper about 'your Wordsley Wonder Pea. I have had in many cases pods with 13 Peas in a pod, and (in one instance only) the, to me, unparalleled number of 14 in a pod.'

A row of garden sheds forms the centrepiece for an exhibition garden at Chaumont-sur-Loire in France.

The garden catalogues, which from the mid-1800s promised dream crops from their products, marketed architectural and garden ornaments designed to lure admiring friends into the kitchen garden. There were fountains for the dipping ponds, sundials, dovecotes and beehives for the walled garden, and follies, glasshouses and rustic summerhouses. There were also potting sheds.

The villa gardener, for example, could spend a profitable Saturday afternoon reconstructing his Portable Hexagon Summer-House (£22), which 'can easily be put together by two persons in one hour'. If he chose to he could specify one of William Cooper's 'Tenant's Fixtures. This house is made in sections and can easily be put together or taken down and removed.' In large Victorian walled gardens the number of outhouses and sheds could run into double figures with potting shed, garden office, seed store, bothy for the water boy and tool shed. But the craft of the shed, or its smarter sister the summer-house, reached its apotheosis on the allotment. Here the potting shed might serve as a retreat from the city slums. In some cases it became the family home itself. David Crouch and Colin Ward in *The Allotment* (1988) record how Nottingham's oldest allotment site at Hunger Hill was dotted with brick-built summerhouses where, in the home-hungry days of the early 1900s, many people lived. One woman had been born there and brought up in a family of eight.

In poor weather Eric Kirten still shelters in his allotment shed on Hunger Hill. Made from recycled planks, old doors and windows and

Eric Kirten outside his potting shed at Nottingham's Hunger Hill allotments.

warmed by a stove, fuelled with cut-up wooden window frames, the scene inside is one of comfortable chaos. The benches are covered with old seed catalogues, seedlings in yoghurt pots and spilled trays of potting compost. 'It's a place of retreat,' explains Eric.

Pest Control

Once upon a time people grew vegetables to stave off starvation. That once-upon-a-time has covered some of the bleakest periods in history, from the Black Death to two world wars. Now, however, many have returned to growing vegetables in the kitchen garden to avoid poisoning their families. In 2002 one survey estimated that 40 per cent of shop-bought vegetables and fruit contained pesticides residues. Jude Cooper has held an allotment in the Welsh border town of Hay-on-Wye for fifteen years. 'Growing our own vegetables is

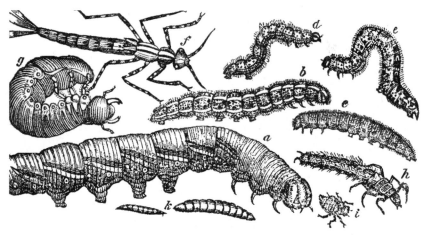

Garden pests from Loudon's *Encyclopaedia of Gardening*. Loudon regarded 'human enemies' as the worst nuisance and recommended using man traps. (*John Loudon, Encyclopaedia of Gardening*)

a form of rest and relaxation and there's a great spirit of camaraderie on the allotments. But above all I can eat what I know – and I know what I grow is free of potentially carcinogenic pesticides.'

A century ago some of the more powerful pesticides used to boost productivity were from natural sources, as former head gardener Keith Ruck recalled: 'Nicotine was our main thing for all insecticides and green sulphur for fungi diseases. You bought nicotine liquid from the chemist or you bought nicotine shreds for fumigating the greenhouses. These were tobacco leaves cut up and soaked with nicotine to make them extra deadly. You'd put six heaps in the conservatory and light them. By the time you got to light the last it would be getting a bit strong in there.'

Outside the glasshouse the garden writer Shirley Hibberd advocated a drenching of laurel water to eradicate caterpillars from the brassica tribe. Alternatively 'hand-picking is very effectual and not so endless a job as it may appear'. He would dip the roots of brassica transplants into a puddle of soot and lime to protect against club root (a century later gardeners used a solution of disinfectant in the same way) and would loose a 'brood of young ducks – the best vermin destroyer' to clean up the cabbage patch.

In John Loudon's book the worst pests in the garden were 'the human enemies . . . such as break in secretly to steal clandestinely'. He recommended that 'the dog is most effectual', but also considered 'man-traps, spring-guns, and alarums . . . have considerable influence'. One commentator of the Middle Ages declared: 'wormes that . . . waster my herbes, I dash them to death.' Loudon too waged war on the friendly worm, insisting on 'gathering by hand all worms, snails, slugs, grubs, and other insects, as soon as they appear'.

Other products of the 1800s included plant-based powders and sprays derived from derris, tobacco, hellebore, pyrethrum and quassia. Home-made recipes for camphor, soft soap, sulphur and

A Dutch scarecrow guards the garden at the Floriade festival in Holland.

turpentine coped with mealy bugs and white scale, while smouldering laurel leaves put paid to green- and whitefly.

Avaricious birds were kept at bay by the scarecrow, at first a gibbet hung with a dead bird, and later a mannequin dressed in old clothes from jumble sales, and seeds coated in red lead paint. Arsenic was added to the list of poisons used against unwanted pests both inside and outside the garden: one Hay-on-Wye solicitor, Major Herbert Armstrong, was hanged in 1922 for poisoning his wife with arsenic intended for the garden.

In America in the 1940s, meanwhile, the tobacco-based Black Leaf 40 was a sure protection against most bugs, while mothballs, nicotine sprays and pyrethrum entered the human food chain as they were routinely applied to vegetables. Another handy chemical in the garden shed was calcium cyanide gas, useful for dealing with burrowing woodchucks, chipmunks and rats.

By the end of the Second World War a chemical armoury, developed for commercial market gardeners and vegetable farmers, was filtering down to the backyard gardener. The carnage in the kitchen garden continued through the 1900s, although there were some milder alternatives. The British Ministry of Agriculture, for example, recommended derris dust as being especially effective with the flea beetle. For those who felt uneasy about chemical killing there was a mechanical aid available – the greased flea beetle wheel. This was a home-made circle of cardboard, pinned to a cane and plastered with the thick grease normally reserved to lubricate the moving parts on the family's Vauxhall Victor. The theory was sound: as the gardener pushed the greased unicycle along the row of affected beetroot, the alarmed flea beetle leapt, as only fleas do, struck the card and stuck fast. (I tried it as a jobbing gardener in the early 1970s. It was a failure.)

However, the British garden writer Stuart Dudley ('the only good weed is a dead weed') reflected the general view of the post-war vegetable-grower. 'Let it not be said in this jet age of today that the gardeners of England are fighting the Weed War of today with the weapons of Napoleon,' he wrote in 1962 in *Taking the Ache out of Gardening*. 'Our back-room boys have provided the wherewithal to blot out the whole of the plant and insect kingdom – let us use them with due circumspection.' The implication was clear: the boffins must know what they were doing and the gardener should carry on with the battle, albeit with care.

By the 1960s, there were signs that horticultural and agricultural chemical warfare was damaging the environment. In his seminal *The Complete Book of Self Sufficiency* (1976), John Seymour offered a practical approach to the recurring, utopian dream of the back-to-the-landers. 'The true homesteader will seek to husband his land, not exploit it,' he wrote. 'He will realize that if he interferes with the chain of life (of which he is a part) he does so at his peril, for he cannot avoid disturbing a natural balance.' The sensitive gardener would 'always get pests and diseases but they will not reach serious proportions', he wrote, advocating a holistic and essentially benevolent approach to growing vegetables.

The Slug and Snail War

Two thousand years of pest control has failed to resolve a problem that has vexed gardeners since kitchen gardening began: slugs and snails. 'Sowed a pint more of dwarf kidney beans in the room of those that were devoured by snails,' wrote a morose Gilbert White in 1759.

Here is the accumulated wisdom of 2,000 years of gardening.

60–65	Lucius Junius Moderatus Columella suggested a sacrifice 'with blood and entrails of a sucking whelp'.
Date unknown	Sprinkle ashes 'from the public baths' around sensitive plants.

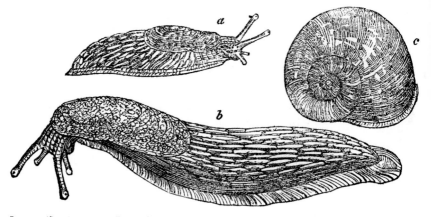

From sacrifices to copper collars. The gardener has waged a long and unsuccessful war on slugs and snails. (*John Loudon, Encyclopaedia of Gardening*)

1000	An Arab gardener in Spain recommends laying cabbage leaves under which slugs and snails shelter at night. In the early morning the gardener can dispose of them.
1400	Dropping slugs in a mix of ashes and unslaked lime.
Date unknown	A Londoner is reported to be keeping four pet seagulls to deal with these 'little beasts injurious to kitchen gardens'.
1571	Kitchen garden paths are watered with an infusion of walnut leaves, salt and crushed shells.
1760	Crushed tobacco leaves are added to the toxic infusion above.
1820	'Annoy them' by scattering caustic substances over them or by watering them with bitter infusions such as vinegar or lime water.
1850	Hand pick them from beneath decaying leaves or haulms laid down as lures.

1870	Quick lime is sprinkled on slugs.
1900	Plants should be encircled with zinc collars.
1920	Slugs are sprinkled with salt.
1930	Surrounding plants with prickly barley straw heads is recommended.
1930s	Ducklings should be let in to the vegetable garden to forage for slugs and snails.
1950	Place heaps of a mixture of metaldehyde and bran or tea leaves around the attacked crop on a warm evening when the soil is moist. Cover the heaps with wood or grass.
1970	Hand collect slugs and snails and deposit them in a bucket filled with creosote-flavoured water.
1977	Lawrence D. Hills unveils the slug trap. 'The traditional soup plate, wide and shallow, sunk level with the ground and filled with a mixture of 1 part of beer to 2 of water, sweetened with 1 dessert-spoonful of Barbados sugar to 1 pt of the mixture.' Hills, who also advocated keeping a hedgehog, reported the capture of 60,000 slugs in one garden in a year.
1980	Metaldehyde slug baits, formed into pellets and scattered around susceptible plants.
1990	Collecting slugs and snails by hand and throwing them over the garden wall. Or transporting them by car to a different neighbourhood – but amateur experiments marking snails shells with paint suggested the snail had good homing instincts.
2002	Perhaps the best advice is that of gardener Rick Guest: 'Each evening I go around collecting them by hand and then I return them to where they belong and where they are happy to live – the compost heap.'

Mr Henry Doubleday's Solution

In the 1970s, when John Seymour's *The Complete Book of Self Sufficiency* was published, E.F. Schumaker, author of *Small is Beautiful*, voiced the concerns of a new generation in his introduction to Seymour's book. People, he warned, were overdependent on fantastic machinery and on larger and larger incomes. 'They may claim to be more highly educated than any generation before them, but the fact remains they cannot really do anything for themselves.' In the vegetable garden, at least, that was about to change.

The Soil Association, founded to promote organic growing, had been set up in 1943 by society girl turned organic farmer, Eve Balfour, after she had published her best seller, *The Living Soil*. It promoted the organic cause and influenced the publication in 1962 of Rachael Carson's *Silent Spring*, her title a reference to what the future held if nations continued to poison their soil with fertilisers and pesticides.

In the 1950s a freelance journalist, Lawrence Hills, decided to experiment with growing organic vegetables and fruit and to improve ways of growing them organically. In the pre-war dictionaries organic meant 'pertaining to the animal and vegetable worlds; forming a whole with a systematic arrangement of parts'. In the 1960s, as Hills explained, it was invested with a new and potent meaning. An organic gardener would be one who had given up chemical fertilisers, pesticides and herbicides. 'Some [gardeners] change on ethical grounds to stop pollution harmful to birds, bees and men, others to save money, since it is easy even at today's vegetable prices to spend more on chemicals than you save when growing your own food,' he wrote in 1977. Hills had read about experiments with comfrey conducted by a nineteenth-century Quaker Henry Doubleday and he wanted to find out more about the use of comfrey as an organic aid.

In the 1870s Doubleday, who ran a small gum factory, had experienced difficulties sourcing his usual gum arabic. When he heard that prickly comfrey (*Symphytum asperum*), a native of the Caucasus, was reputed to contain much 'mucilaginous matter', he wrote to the gardener at the palace of St Petersburg in Russia requesting some plants. Doubleday hoped to extract a glue from the comfrey for use on postage stamps.

The gardener sent Russian comfrey (*Symphytum X uplandicum*) by mistake. A natural hybrid, the Russian comfrey was no use for gum, but Doubleday, who was also a smallholder, realised its potential as a fodder crop. He set out to improve the variety by selecting the best plants with the highest yields. This was not long after the Irish potato famine and Doubleday wanted to develop a crop that could save the world from famine and starvation.

When Hills rented an acre of land at Bocking near Braintree in Essex, he set up his own trials to investigate and categorise the different forms of British comfrey. He named the comfrey cultivars after the Bocking trial grounds. 'Comfrey,' he wrote in his classic *Organic Gardening*, 'is so rich in protein . . . that it is a kind of instant compost. It has roots that go down 4–8 feet, which is deeper than most fruit trees, but instead of locking up the minerals in the wood where only fire and fungi can release them, it keeps them all in a 'current account', as it were, ready for immediate use by crops.'

The Quaker gardener Mr Henry Doubleday was the inspiration for the modern organic movement. (*Henry Doubleday Research Association*)

His leading variety for the kitchen garden was Bocking

167

A Good Idea at the Time
Soil Conditioner

'Peat is excellent for lightening heavy soils, and when black and decomposed is just right for manuring purposes,' promised one gardening writer in the 1950s.

British gardeners took up the promise, improving their soil with peat from the dense carpets of vegetation gradually laid down in Ireland since the last Ice Age 10,000 years ago.

Irish peat proved so popular that, despite the warnings of conservationists alarmed by the scale of the damage to the peat bogs, UK gardeners were still buying around two million cubic metres of Irish peat in 2000.

Now over 90 per cent of Ireland's raised bogs have been damaged by the gardening trade. Experts have predicted that an area the size of an entire Irish county could be left barren by the year 2010.

14, 'a semi-sterile hybrid between *Symphytum asperum* from Russia and the wild *Symphytum officinale*, the herbalists' comfrey'. Hills founded an organisation to spread the word – and the comfrey – naming it after the Quaker, the Henry Doubleday Research Association, HDRA. A networking group that relied on feedback from its member gardeners, it grew quickly. By the start of the 1970s, there were 17,000 members sharing their own ideas on organic gardening, while Hills's wife, Cherry, shared her thoughts

Lawrence D. Hills, with his wife Cherry, founder of the Henry Doubleday Research Association. (*Henry Doubleday Research Association*)

on vegetable nutrition: she raised early concerns, for example, of the possible link between aluminium cooking pans and Alzheimer's disease.

As the organisation grew, two young scientists, Alan and Jackie Gear, responded to an advertisement in *The Times*: 'Young couple wanted to work on an organic research station. Full board. No pay' and joined HDRA. In the 1980s, as Lawrence Hills handed the running of the organisation over to the Gears, the couple moved HDRA to its new home, then a run-down, wind-swept 22-acre smallholding near Coventry at Ryton-on-Dunsmore.

Hills died in the 1990s, but not before he had seen HDRA, with a membership of around 30,000, become the largest organic organisation in Europe, with the future King of England, the Prince of Wales, as its patron. Ryton was now home to sample organic gardens devoted to ornamental vegetables, different methods of growing vegetables and a children's vegetable patch. There were other exhibition plots at Yalding in Kent and the vegetable garden at Audely End had been restored. HDRA had set up a heritage seed library to rescue old and odd vegetable varieties and was supporting farmers in developing countries to grow organic vegetables. 'Provided we do not drive our soils too hard, the land will go on feeding us through the sunlit centuries when motoring is but a memory,' Hills had predicted. HDRA had set out to show how it could be done.

5

Vegetable Bounty

A Vegetable Herbal
The Vegetarian Movement
To the Market
London's Larder
Vegetables Preserved
A Vegetable Calendar

A Vegetable Herbal

If the biblical Garden of Eden, with its temptingly forbidden fruit, was a place of paradise, the down-to-earth kitchen garden was a place of healing. John Gerard, for example, thought the lettuce 'cooleth the heat of the stomacke, called the heart-burning; and helpeth it when it is troubled with choler; it quencheth thirst, and causeth sleepe'. The fruit of the cucumber, meanwhile, 'cut in pieces or chopped as herbes to the pot' and taken three times a day, 'doth perfectly cure all manner of sauce flegme and copper faces, red and shining fieries noses . . . and such like precious faces'.

Much of the information about the vegetable herbal reached Europe from Africa and the Middle East. Following their invasion of Persia in the seventh century, Arab conquerors absorbed rather than destroyed the civilised Persian gardens, which were stocked with useful plants. The Moors carried this horticultural knowledge and their pharmaceutical texts with them as they moved up through Spain in the 800s and introduced their own citrus fruits and 'new' vegetables such as cauliflowers, red-rooted carrots, cardoons, aubergines and artichokes. Artichokes were a celebrated aphrodisiac, but the aubergine had mysterious properties: while Moors could consume them with impunity, it was said that Christians risked death if they ate them.

This sometimes suspect knowledge was carried through Europe, especially in the royal courts: kings and queens naturally expected to benefit from the very latest medical opinions. Scholars, too, passed on the plant pharmacology from monastery to monastery. Here in the medieval hierarchy God was the chief physician, although the monk might do what he could to alleviate suffering. The infirmarer (the term 'infirmary', carried to the New World by the founding fathers, outlived its use in Europe) expected his gardeners in the infirmary garden to be able to identify, cultivate and prepare medicinal concoctions for his patients and convalescing monks. Stress is nothing new; bled six times a year to alleviate stress, the monks would afterwards receive nourishing vegetables from the abbey gardens and be allowed the quiet stimulation of conversation in the pleasant surroundings of the parlour (from *parler* to talk). On the subject of bleeding, a male horror of menstruation led some to advocate that a woman 'in her terms' should not enter the melonry for fear that the fruit would drop off. Early 'authorities' declared that, if a young woman, menstruating for the first time, was led around the cabbage patch, it would kill any caterpillars on the crop. But the gardener had to take care: young plants would die if a woman in menstruation so much as looked at them.

The monastic arsenal of medicinal plants included herbs, spices and vegetables. No distinction was made between vegetables and other medicinal plants until the mid 1700s – everything that grew in the kitchen garden was thought to have healthy properties. The apothecary advocated diets of salads and healing vegetables for the 'pottage' while the yeoman and his wife grew a steady supply of herbal plants and vegetables in the garden – there is nothing new in the idea of a healthy diet.

From the Middle Ages to the late 1800s physicians took a holistic approach to their patients' ills, advocating good air, exercise, rest and, on the premiss that a little of what you fancy does you good, a modicum of strong emotions such as pleasure or anxiety. A mother, meanwhile, relied on her hand-me-down knowledge and experience to care for a sick child or relative. She would be familiar with hedgerow cures, treating worms with vermicidal plants such as mugwort or wormwood, for example, or prescribing salads, pottages and tisanes (an infusion of dried herbs) for a particular condition. Until the 1400s, however, she could update that knowledge only from hearsay, since her gender kept her in a state of illiteracy, particularly of the *lingua medicina*, the language of medicine, Latin.

Gradually these Latin texts were translated, and pirated copies were circulated around the country homes.

So it was she learned that the wild parsnip in a decoction helped the bowels to move and the urine to flow, while oil extracted from the seeds could soothe intermittent fevers such as malaria. From Thomas Hill's *Gardener's Labyrinth* (1577) she discovered even greater benefits: 'Parsnep removeth the venereal act, procureth Urine, and asswageth the Cholerick, sendeth down the Termes in Women; it profiteth the Melanchollicke, encreaseth good blood, helpeth the straightnese of making water, amendeth stitches of the sides or purisies, the bite of venemous beast, it amendeth the eating of Ulcers, the wearing of this root is profitable.' You might feel foolish wearing your *parsnep*, but at least you knew it was doing you good.

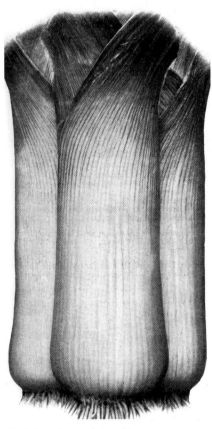

The leek, made into a hot poultice, was a certain cure for inflammations of the arm. (*Suttons Consumer Products Ltd*)

The leek featured as a cure for an inflammation of the arm if it was used as a hot poultice. If the housewife could plan ahead, she might take advantage of the knowledge that celery boiled with oil and sweet beer and swallowed four days in a row acted as a contraceptive. It would treat

Rheumatism could be kept in check by a stolen potato. (*Suttons Consumer Products Ltd*)

bloodshot eyes if mixed with resinous frankincense and, mixed with any oil, was a salve for sore joints. Wild celery was a laxative and diuretic, relieving swellings and breaking up gallstones. For the prevention of kidney stones, seakale was the answer, according to the apothecary William Curtis in 1799. The up-and-coming potato had its uses too. Early potatoes fetched a high price as an aphrodisiac, while a potato was a sure charm against rheumatism – but only if it had been stolen. A slice of potato rubbed over a wart and then buried caused the wart to disappear.

Garlic was used as an antiseptic during the First World War, while the onion was a prophetic vegetable: the thickening of onion skins was a sure sign of a bad winter approaching.

Leaf vegetables were always useful. (Parsley, as we have seen from Peter Rabbit's native knowledge, was a cure for stomach ache. Less well known, except to the Romans, was the idea that parsley could cure sick fish if scattered on the surface of the pond.) Since lettuce, the sacred plant of the Egyptian goddess of fertility, was used in sacrifices, it was forbidden food for the temple priests. For the laity, however, it made a healing poultice and could cure stomach aches and coughs. While Greeks and Romans ate their lettuces last thing at night to calm the mind and induce sleep, the lettuce also promised to cleanse the blood, promote milk in nursing mothers, cure excessive drinking and counter impotence. (The Romans believed that eating raw, pickled cabbage before a meal countered the effects of alcohol.)

The bean was another life-saver. Henry Thoreau noted a Roman passion for beans – 'not that I wanted beans to eat, for I am by nature a Pythagorean, so far as beans are concerned, whether they mean porridge or voting', he explained in 1845. (The Greek Pythagoreans, believing that the soul passed on into another body after death, had an aversion to the foetal-shaped beans, which seemed to presage the germ of life. Roman politicians, on the other hand, preferred to distribute free beans to bolster their chances at the polls.) The Celts supposedly celebrated with a beanfeast, Scottish witches reputedly rode not broomsticks, but beanstalks, and it was expedient to carry a bean or two with you on dark nights: ghosts were sent packing if you spat a bean at them. Gerard noted that the pea was 'not so windy as be the beans', but there were fraudulent overtones to giving a man 'a pea for a bean'. Religious customs had plenty of uses for the vegetable crop. Onions, leeks and colewort were dutifully eaten during Lent, while carlin peas, grown in the north-east of England, were soaked overnight and eaten on Passion or Carlin Sunday. Whether this was a religious rite or a stopgap meal at a time of year when the vegetable plot was depleted is not recorded.

Although Pliny the Elder had recorded no less than eighty-seven cabbage-related medicines, the general view of vegetables through the 1700s and 1800s was that, while they might cure you of one or two ailments, they were basically not to be trusted. In the Elizabethan age, for example, the potentially healthy benefits of vegetables were lost on the sailing fraternity, who rarely listed fresh vegetables among their ships' provisions. On board, a diet of dried beans was bad enough, without adding beetroot, which was said to cause flatulence. Dysentery and malaria were said to be symptoms, not of contaminated water or mosquitoes, but of the wholly innocent cucumber. Nicholas Culpeper, meanwhile, had already condemned that other salad crop, the radish, in his *Compleat Herbal* of 1652: 'Garden radishes are in wantonness by the gentry eaten as a salad, but they breed but scurvy humours in the stomach, and corrupt the blood, and then send for a physician as fast as you can,' he advised.

Not until the 1800s did the Admiralty accept the necessity of dosing its sailors with lemon juice to counter scurvy. In the interests of economy, however, they carried the cheaper, and less effective, limes from the British colonies; ever after the British sailor was referred to as a limey by the Americans. But by the mid-1800s attitudes to vegetables were changing on both sides of the Atlantic. 'The garden pays full as well as the field,' advised one North American farmer in a periodical of 1859. Twenty years on a Mr Hood was corresponding with the *Canadian Horticulturalist* on the healthy benefits of eating tomatoes and increasing 'one's hopes of longevity. How glorious a thing to be able, like Macbeth, to say 'Throw physic to the dogs', and rejoice in the diminution of your doctor's bills.'

In Europe too the vegetable news was good, at least according to this commentator, writing for Sutton's seed catalogue of 1881. 'The potato' has contributed in a wonderful degree to the reformation of the national dietary, so that, while the masses are better fed, so they are less familiar with scrofula and scurvy, and as for "plagues and pestilences" of the older sort, they appear to be banished out of civil society, and the average length of life of the whole population appears to increase from year to year.'

However, there was no room for complacency. In 1899 the British nation needed healthy recruits for the war against the Boers. The average farmhand was found to be fit enough to fight, but several thousand urban volunteers had to be rejected because their slum-city diets kept them in a state of permanent ill health.

It took two world wars to drive home the message that greens were good for you. 'Gardens are still in the news', wrote a Toronto columnist Collier Stevenson in 1943, 'for . . . the raising of vitamin- and mineral-rich vegetables, both for the nutritional and economic advantage to Canada.'

The postwar argument in North America concerned not the healthy benefits or otherwise of the vegetable, but the kitchen gardener's position: was he an organic gardener or a chemical gardener? During the dustbowl disaster of 1935, thousands of tons of top soil were blown off the heavily fertilised fields of the American West, ruining many farmers. The catastrophe triggered the beginnings of a crisis of confidence between the consumer and the chemical fertiliser industry. The insistent campaigns of New Yorker Jerome I. Rodale (the *New York Times* called him the 'Guru of the Organic Food Cult') and his *Organic Gardening* magazine, Rachel Carson's book, *Silent Spring*, and growing concerns over sources of environmental pollution from nuclear fallout to farm pesticides moved the argument along in favour of the organic gardener.

It was not long before an alternative shop, designed to cater specifically for those who were worried about their health, was slipping into the back streets, the wholefood and health-food store.

In the UK, when a free health service was being offered to the nation in the aftermath of the Second World War, Western medicine placed its faith firmly in pharmaceuticals and surgery. The herbalists, who, before the war, had traded on every high street in the country, packed up their plants and potions and went away, taking with them twenty centuries of wisdom. And yet, while 25 per cent of the world's medicines were based on plant extracts, only an estimated 10 per cent of the world's species of plants had been properly analysed.

Within twenty years the vegetable remedies were back, filling the shelves of the new breed of health stores that had crossed over from America. When, in 2003, Dr John Briffa was telling the readers of his column in the *Observer* magazine that 'the onion

Spinach may not have made Popeye stronger, but it would have worked wonders for his eyesight.

packs an eye-watering nutritional punch', he was repeating the views of ancient Indian, Egyptian, Chinese and Roman physicians centuries before. One vegetable whose healthy benefits were unknown to the Greek and Roman medics was spinach. It arrived from Persia in the sixth century, but the American Elzie Segar had no doubts about its healthy properties when he began sketching out a cartoon character to woo Castor Oyl. This was the muscle-bound hero, Popeye the Sailor Man, who was 'strong to the finich, 'cos I eat me spinach'.

Spinach (we now know) is rich in lutein and zeaxanthin, which, like the more familiar betacarotene, are antioxidants that help to

---

THE TOP FIVE

VEGETABLE APHRODISIACS

1. Artichokes
2. Potatoes – but only early varieties.
3. Lettuce – useful as a cure for impotence.
4. The *pomme d'amour* or tomato.
5. The turnip: 'it augmenteth the seed of man and provoketh carnal lust,' insisted Sir Thomas Elliot in 1539

---

combat free radicals, the molecules that are especially damaging to the proteins in the lens of the human eye and contribute to eye cataracts. Popeye, with his fine eyesight, was appropriately, if inadvertently, named.

The Vegetarian Movement

'We must cultivate our garden,' Voltaire declared in his *Candide*, published in 1759. He had a special interest in the contents of the vegetable patch, since he and others including the poets, Alexander Pope and Percy Bysshe Shelley and the pastor John Wesley, promoted the virtues of a meat-free diet. No one took them very seriously until 1847, when a group of Christians and physicians met up at a hospital in Ramsgate, Kent to form the Vegetarian Society. The group included the Horsells, who ran the hospital on vegetarian lines, and the MP for Salford, Joseph Brotherton and his wife Martha, and they took their name from the same Latin root as the vegetable: *vegere*, to enliven and to animate.

Later that year the Manchester branch of the society was launched with a celebratory meal of onion and sage fritters, savoury pie and plum pudding. The recipes were based on the first non-flesh cookery book, which had been published in 1821 by Martha Brotherton after her encounter with the oddly named Revd William Cowherd.

The Salford clergyman abhorred the eating of flesh. He took to the streets with his soup kitchen, distributing free vegetable soup to the poor and earnestly preaching a philosophy of 'live and let live' to his congregation at the Bible Christian Church. At a time

The Revd Cowherd, an early advocate of the vegetarian diet, preached the cause with missionary zeal. (*The Vegetarian Society*)

when meat was expensive and food scares common, he gained a significant following. Converts went to America, where Amos Bronson Alcott, father of Louisa May Alcott, the author of *Little Women*, and neighbour of Henry Thoreau, and a biscuit manufacturer Sylvester Graham (who espoused a diet of raw food only) founded the American Vegetarian Society in 1850. The movement attracted many nineteenth-century celebrities, including Annie Besant (who founded the influential Theosophical Society), the shorthand inventor Isaac Pitman, the Russian novelist Leo Tolstoy, Mahatma Gandhi and novelist and playwright George Bernard Shaw. The Vegetarians, however, were not so much pro-vegetable eaters as anti-meat. 'Animals are my friends and I don't eat my friends,' explained Shaw.

To the Market

Every spring avalanches of green artichokes and asparagus cascade across the marble counters of the *Modernismo* market hall in Valencia. In Amsterdam's Boerenmarkt, red, green and yellow tomatoes, peppers and aubergines are arranged in Rastafarian-coloured patterns. Fat, ripe pumpkins surround farm pick-ups at a Kingston, Canada country market in the Fall. Fresh vegetables always make a pretty picture, but nothing quite matches the French village market. This is a nation that knows its onions. From the summer run of Citroën vans laden with tomatoes, early potatoes and *haricots verts* in le Midi to the autumn harvest of the Basque pimento, sold to be hung out to dry on the half-timbered house

From Manchester to Morocco, vegetables have been sold at market for centuries. All that is changing fast.

fronts, the French are past masters at bringing their vegetables fresh to market.

The freshest vegetables are those with the shortest journey between kitchen garden and kitchen table, the home-grown variety. Most households, however, must rely on markets and shops for their fresh vegetables. Some of the produce people buy has travelled a long way. Leeks, deflagged (with their tops cut) so they fit their plastic containers, are trucked across country from the Lincolnshire fields to a distribution centre in south-east England and then driven back to the Lincolnshire supermarkets for sale. Some estimates of the amount of road freight dedicated to the distribution of food in the UK have put the figure at over 35 per cent.

Meanwhile bunches of beans, ruler-straight and measuring no more than 95mm so they fit perfectly their cling-filmed plastic trays, arrive by air from Kenya. Christmas peas and Easter carrots wing their way to Britain from South Africa, a journey of nearly 6,000 miles, while sugar snap peas arrive, out of season in the UK, from Guatemala. Cheap overseas labour has resulted in some extravagant vegetable journeys: one supermarket chain used to retail attractive trays of miniature vegetables tied with a blade of chives. But before they reached the chilled supermarket shelf, packaging and chives were first flown out of the UK to Kenya's Nairobi airport. Here local women tied the green blades of chives around a selection of Kenyan-grown vegetables before the finished packages were returned by air to the UK.

As the quantity of packaging in the average British dustbin rose to 60 per cent, environmentalists began to protest that the price of the global vegetable market was over-reliant on non-renewable resources and a price too high to pay. In the late 1900s, as the USA began to market the first genetically modified tomato (its inactive ripening gene left it looking fit and well long after it had been harvested), restaurateurs and cooks complained that produce was

Zimbabweans load fresh vegetables and live hens on a bus going to market in Bulawayo. Developed countries use Africa's cheap labour pool to grow vegetables for export.

selected more for its shape, size, and colour rather than for its smell and taste. Supermarkets countered that the seasonless vegetable was a product of consumer choice. The rise of the supermarket to supremacy in the vegetable market place seemed to support their claims: in the 1970s, wholesalers marketed 90 per cent of vegetables and fruit in the UK. Thirty years later the supermarkets had taken over 80 per cent of the market share. And their share was growing.

Supermarkets have proved to be successful hucksters in edging out their rivals, but there is nothing novel about competitive practices in the vegetable market. During the reign of Elizabeth I, for example, housewives were being persuaded to buy new, improved peas, sold green rather than dreary dry for winter storage.

Long journey times for vegetables are nothing new either. The Emperor Tiberius is said to have had his parsnips imported to Rome from the banks of the Rhine in Germany. And before it was removed because of the 'scurrility, clamour and nuisance of the gardeners and their servants', the fourteenth-century market near London's St Paul's, where the 'gardeners of earls, barons, bishops and citizens sold their produce', was provisioned by foot, sail power and the plodding packhorse. The ridgeways, drove roads and salt ways of England carried a steady traffic of cabbage-mongers, garlic-mongers and leek-mongers heading for market with baskets and trays of vegetables for sale.

During the hungry gap between the end of winter and the harvesting of their first vegetables, the poor were entitled by law to pick green peas in the field for their own consumption: hucksters were regularly reprimanded for trying to sell their pickings at market. A more reliable supplier was the local monastery garden, until Henry VIII sequestered the wealth of the monasteries and redistributed it amongst his friends. The Cistercian order, founded in 1098 in Burgundy, France, advocated self-sufficiency in the garden and invested time and effort in good tools and efficient growing methods. The cellarer at Westminster's convent garden, for example, had to supply the monastery with fresh vegetables and herbs, hay for the floors and the *garderobes*, and rushes, mints and meadowsweet for strewing across floors. He had to look after his hedged plots, his house cows and their pasture, and his hives of bees for the honey and wax. There was always surplus produce to be sold at market or traded for seed and cuttings.

The vegetable gardens of 'earls, barons and bishops' also played their part. Head gardeners were often expected to supplement their income with the sale of surplus produce. At Stow Bardolph in Norfolk a contract for the head gardener of 1712 stipulated that he 'maintain and keep and furnish . . . Stow Hall . . . with all necessary and sufficient kitchen garden stuffe'. It also allowed him to pocket the profits from the sale of vegetables to top up his wage of £50 a year.

Vegetables were traded from country to country too. Vegetables had been shipped from France and the Low Countries across to England as early as the 1300s. One of the popular destinations was the old Westminster 'convent' garden, now Covent Garden and one of several markets that claimed to be London's larder.

Inland journey times between the market garden and the market were driven down as roads, carts and carriages improved. They improved even more when, in the 1820s, 3,000 miles of new canal were added to the nation's transport network. The canals also improved the fertility of neighbouring fields and gardens. 'Fields, which before were barren, are now drained, and by the assistance of manure, conveyed on the canal toll-free, are clothed with a beautiful verdure,' Thomas Pennant noted in 1782 of the land around the new Grand Junction Canal between Trent and Mersey.

The railways were hard on its heels. By the 1850s the Scottish laird wintering in the south for the London season could, and did, expect the produce of his walled kitchen garden to be picked, packed and put on the train to London so that it might arrive on the doorstep of his Chelsea villa in a matter of hours. The transport of vegetables – and everything else – was revolutionised.

'Crowds of people and mountains of goods, departing and arriving scores upon scores of times in every four-and-twenty hours, produced a fermentation in the place that was always in action,' wrote Charles Dickens as he watched the Camden Town railway develop in 1836. 'There were railway patterns in its drapers' shops, and railway journals in the windows of its newsmen. There were railway hotels, office-houses, lodging-houses, boarding-houses; railway plans, maps, views, wrappers, bottles, sandwich-boxes, and time-tables.' The 'dunghills, dustheaps, and ditches and gardens, and summerhouses' of the area, meanwhile, had disappeared, as families moved out of town, along the lifeline of the railway, to settle in the country and grow their vegetables there.

Not that the railways were welcomed with open arms. Some were as bitterly opposed as any twentieth-century motorway. 'We are too much hurrying about in these islands; much for idle pleasure, and more from over activity in the pursuit of wealth, without regard to the good or happiness of others,' mourned the poet and vegetable-grower William Wordsworth when plans were announced for a line from Kendal to his favourite Lake Windermere.

What was done was not to be undone (at least until one Dr Beeching radically reduced the railway network in the 1960s). Manufacturers promoted their proximity to the railways: 'The facilities we have on all hands – sea, canal, and rail – for despatching Manures of our usual high standard . . . enable us to ensure the prompt delivery of all orders with which we may be favoured,' promised Webbs of Stourbridge. Markets adjusted their working hours to coincide with the train deliveries and, for a century, railway traffic reigned supreme as small agricultural armies of pickers were formed in the shires to pick the vegetables fresh and send them by the wagon and cart load to the station. Gypsies and travellers followed the ripening crops from region to region and swelled the ranks of local women and children picking for the markets. In the 1970s, one Shropshire man recalled his childhood summer holidays spent picking fruit and vegetables. 'You used to be off school for four weeks picking to buy shoes and clothes to go back to school because your parents couldn't afford them. The produce used to be put in baskets and sent at night on the mail train to Birmingham, to the market there'.

In post-war Britain conditions for the vegetable-pickers were little better, as one former soldier recalled. Returning to East Anglia, he joined a Government agricultural scheme, which gave him work on a local market garden. 'In the army we'd dreamed of returning to "blighty" and perhaps running a little country pub somewhere. Instead I found myself picking Brussel sprouts for the London train, in driving snow up on the cliff top above West Runton and crying with the cold. It was all hand work and in all weathers. We had a horse drawn hoe for the currant crop, but carrots and turnips were hoed out by hand, and beet was topped and tailed with a sickle.' Both the Shropshire lad and the demobbed soldier were picking fruit and vegetables for the bustling city vegetable market. But by the end of the twentieth century most fresh vegetables were being sent instead to supermarket distribution centres.

Supermarkets had started off quietly enough. In 1869 John Sainsbury and his wife established a shop in Drury Lane, just down the road from the Covent Garden market. One hundred and thirty years later, his business had become the third largest supermarket chain in the UK. In the early 1900s Jack Cohen, a young barrow boy, was working in the London markets. He turned a small profit selling surplus army rations and then in 1924 bought a supply of tea from one T.E. Stockwell, sold it again at a profit and founded a small company using the initial letters of his tea supplier with his own surname to create the name Tesco. A visit to America convinced him that the self-service store was the thing of the future and that extending his lines to include non-foodstuffs would create a kind of 'super market'.

As the new generation of Sainsburys and Cohens firmed up their global networks of fresh vegetables, the trend was clear: the high-street greengrocers and the neighbourhood shop were in free fall. Their numbers in the UK, 113,000 in 2003, had dropped by almost 20 per cent in ten years: during the same decade the floor space of the major supermarkets had increased by 50 per cent. Fruit and vegetables were a profitable trade and one worth competing for. With an average mark-up of 40 per cent on fruit and vegetables, the

How fresh is it? A French *grandmère* selects the freshest produce at an open market in Brittany.

produce aisle of the supermarket was now the most lucrative part of the store. But the worldwide market, created to fill the shelves as profitably as possible, had its critics. One was the Indian activist Vandana Shiva, who claimed that a global monoculture was being forced on people 'by defining everything that is fresh, local and handmade as a health hazard. Human hands are being defined as the worst contaminants, and work for human hands is being outlawed, to be replaced by machines and chemicals bought from global corporations.' Supporters of her views, insisting that quality was being sacrificed for quantity, spurned the supermarkets and patronised farm shops, local markets and vegetable box schemes, where householders bought only locally available vegetables that were in season. Time will tell whether the small, local vegetable producer will survive or go to the wall under pressure from the supermarket supremacy in fresh veg.

London's Larder

Covent Garden was once the largest fruit and vegetable market in the UK. Until the 1600s, grain grew in the fields, and vegetables in the gardens, that surrounded the convent of St Peter of Westminster. The convent had been built on an old Saxon site, part of a ninth-century settlement called Lundenwic and one that was regularly threatened by Viking invaders sailing up river to plunder the town. The convent grounds declined after the dissolution of the monasteries by Henry VIII in the 1500s, until a London developer, the Earl of Bedford, proposed a radical experiment in early town planning. With the enthusiastic support of King Charles I, the Earl

Red, green and yellow tomatoes, peppers and aubergines create geometric patterns on a market stall.

190

London's larder, Covent Garden market, finally closed in 1974. Now the vegetable stalls have been replaced by tourists.

persuaded the most important architect of his day, Inigo Jones, to design a public square. Drawing on his experience of the classical Italian *piazza*, Jones demolished the winding alleys and lanes of the immediate neighbourhood and introduced the formal square to the people of London. As the convent gardens were buried beneath the foundations of the smart new town houses and Jones's classical church of St Paul, the public spilled into the square to admire his work. (Commissioning his church, the Earl is reputed to have told Jones he could scarcely afford a barn, let alone a church. 'My Lord, you shall have the handsomest barn in England,' replied Jones.) Unfortunately for the Earl of Bedford, the public nature of the square was its undoing, and the wealthy, having so recently moved in, were soon moving away again to more private, neighbouring squares.

As the rich moved out, the fruit and vegetables moved in. A small market had stood here in 1649 surrounded by bordellos, coffee houses and Turkish bathing houses. It expanded gradually until, by the 1830s, it could rightfully claim to be the larder of London. At its height Covent Garden employed over 1,000 porters and barrow boys. 'The wall-like regularity with which cabbage, cauliflowers, and turnips are built up to a height of some twelve feet is nothing short of marvellous,' reported an enthusiastic Charles Dickens. The satirical magazine *Punch*, however, described Covent Garden as 'Mud Salad Market' and 'about the greatest nuisance ever permitted'. In 1886 Covent Garden Market opened a new Floral Hall and market gardeners and country-house head gardeners alike fed the market their produce.

In 1974 the old Garden was finally closed and a new one opened at Nine Elms in Vauxhall. After a battle by conservationists over plans to redevelop the Garden, campaigners won the day, the Secretary of State promised to preserve the main buildings and the Garden was turned into the tourist market it is today.

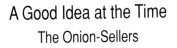

A Good Idea at the Time
The Onion-Sellers

It was an inadvertent, but briefly successful marketing ploy by Breton onion-growers that led to the French stereotype of a garçon *in a striped vest, sailor's trousers and black beret precariously riding a bicycle with a* bâton *of bread or a string of onions across the handlebars.*

Times were hard in Brittany l'entre-deux-guerres (between the two world wars), and nowhere more so than on the north coast of Brittany in the onion-growing region around Trégor. Here the young men wore the Breton beret, and the sailors their striped shirt, just as their fathers and grandfathers had before them. But, unlike their forefathers, the young men were ready to travel and earn some money. In late summer, when the onion crops were gathered in at villages like Yffiniac, near Saint-Brieuc, the young men would borrow the family bike and, carrying as many strings of onions as they could across the handlebars, ride down to the fishing ports of Saint-Brieuc or Tréguier to hitch a ride to the English ports. The traditional journée d'Albion, or journey to Albion, brought early onions to the English south coast in what was mistakenly assumed by the cartoonists of the day to be the traditional French costume.

In 2003 the Breton town of Roscoff announced the opening of a museum dedicated to 'Johnny Onion', as their door-to-door onion salesmen were known.

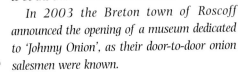

A group of Bretons prepare to embark for England, their cycles buried beneath a cascade of onions. (*Musée des Johnnies, Roscoff*)

Vegetables Preserved

In the early 1800s the French navy, under blockade from the British, set sail from the port of Brest with a secret weapon on board. Hidden below decks were rows of champagne bottles filled, not with fine wine from that region, but beans, peas and boiled beef in gravy. The bottles were kept sealed for three months before they were opened and their contents sampled. While the beef tea was judged rather weak, the beans and peas were considered to have all the freshness and flavour of new picked vegetables – high praise from a nation that traditionally cast a hyper-critical eye on the quality of its vegetables.

The bottles had been prepared by Nicolas Appert, the chef and confectioner who invented the process of canning vegetables, fruit and meat. Born at Chalôns-sur-Marne on the edge of the Champagne region in 1750 where his father worked as a brewer and innkeeper, Appert died in 1841, his culinary contribution all but forgotten. Not until a French postage stamp was issued in his honour in 1955 was M. Appert's genius acknowledged.

Appert had moved to Paris in 1781 and began experimenting with preserving food, filling his champagne bottles with different vegetables, fruit and meat and standing them in hot water before sealing them. After the success of the naval sea trials, Appert, now living at Masy near Paris, set up the world's first canning factory – except that he was still using bottles, specially made to his design and stored in canvas bags to protect his workers from flying glass, should a bottle explode. His little factory was filled with cauldrons and copper boilers, kitchens and cold stores, bottle racks and cork stoppers, all devoted to storing and preserving food in such a way that the consumer could enjoy 'the month of May in the heart of winter', as his patron Grimond de La Reynière put it.

The business went well: forty women worked in the factory during the busy vegetable harvest and Appert's preserves sold in the Paris shops. The commercial potential of Appert's invention began to dawn on French government officials: preserved French vegetables could be sold for export; naval vessels could stay at sea longer; and food would no longer have to be preserved with sugar, which, under the British blockade, was in short supply. Appert, always generous with his research, was commissioned by the government to reveal the secrets of his process. But just as his book, *L'Art de conserver pendant plusiers années toutes les substances animales et végetales*, appeared in 1810, a Londoner, Peter Durand, patented the process, and a London engineering company began preserving food by Appert's methods, using cans rather than bottles. Appert's own

These two little birds think it very unkind that Farrow's should come, and, before they have dined, take all the best peas and the ripe juicy plums, and leave them to beg for the stalest bread crumbs. But there, it is true, as they know in the nest, the peas canned by Farrow's are picked from the best.

FARROW'S
FOR CHOICE
English Canned Fruits and Vegetables

An advertisement for English canned fruit and vegetables. But was the idea stolen from its French inventor, Nicolas Appert?

196

business floundered until, in the 1830s, he found the finance to set up another factory to bottle and can vegetables. By now the competition was too intense; the business failed and Appert died in obscurity and poverty.

The French may have forgotten Appert, but they did not forget his bottled vegetables, still a staple line in French food shops today. Shelves of bottled and canned vegetables, however, were about to make way for a new piece of equipment in the store, the freezer cabinet.

The post-war vegetable, served as 'meat and two veg', was a poor and watery thing. A 1950s author who offered sensible advice on travelling etiquette – 'if talking with strangers leads to further conversation, it should remain impersonal' – also offered useful advice on cooking vegetables: 'Vegetables, Boiling. All vegetables grown above ground should be boiled with the lid off the saucepan whilst those grown under should have the lid kept on.' She was not going to advocate the art of steaming vegetables or celebrating the vegetable in the French fashion, where each course of vegetables was served and savoured separately. New frosted vegetables were about to change all that.

What Eleanor Birdseye missed most about life as a fur-trapper's wife in Labrador in the early years of the 1900s was fresh, green vegetables. She lived with her husband, Clarence, or Bob as he preferred to be called, and their son Kellogg in a three-roomed cabin 250 miles away from the nearest store or doctor. Bob, born in 1886 in New York, dropped out of Amherst College in Massachusetts because his family could not afford the fees. For a brief period he took a job with the US Department of Agriculture, but, always the risk-taker, he persuaded Eleanor that there was a better living to be had from fur trapping. They moved to their lonely shack in north-eastern Canada, where they lived off home-frozen food.

Bob Birdseye learned quickly what the native north Canadians already knew, that meat tasted better if it was frozen fast. Fish, rabbit, duck and other game, naturally frozen outdoors in the Arctic winds that drove the temperatures down as low as −50 °C, kept their flavour. 'The Eskimos had used it for centuries. What I accomplished . . . was merely to make packaged frozen food available to the public,' he would say later.

To please Eleanor, Bob experimented with freezing vegetables. He stored cabbage brought by boat in barrels filled with salt water. 'Fresh' cabbage was then hacked out of the ice when required.

In 1917 the family returned to the USA and Bob Birdseye borrowed the corner of an ice cream works in New Jersey, where, in an effort to 'reproduce the Labrador winters' by means of ice blocks, brine and an electric fan, he set up business selling frozen fish. The business went bust. The Birdseyes moved on, this time to the fishing port of Gloucester, where the tenacious entrepreneur experimented with quick freezing meat, fish and vegetables. He built an automatic freezer that could fast freeze food when it was placed between metal plates that had been cooled to −40 °C with calcium chloride brine. After patenting the process and setting up a new business, the General Seafoods Company, Bob Birdseye concentrated on improving his methods. Convinced of the need to freeze vegetables while they were still fresh, he mobilised his quick freezer, mounting it on the back of a truck and driving it out into the fields, where he could freeze the vegetables as they were picked. But business was slow and, at one point, he and Eleanor had to hock their insurance policies to keep it afloat. It was just as well, since he would shortly receive what was then the largest single sum of money ever paid for a single process, $22 million.

The pay-off came by chance. Marjorie Merryweather Post, the daughter of a food-processing company-owner, was taking a yatching holiday on the Massachusetts coast. One evening her chef served her roast goose bought in Gloucester from the General Seafoods Company. When she learned that the fresh goose was

An inveterate risk-taker, Clarence Birdseye was finally able to retire on the profitable proceeds of his freezing invention. (*Birds Eye Foods*)

actually several months old, she made an appointment to see Bob Birdseye. Three years later Bob's company was bought out by her family's firm and in 1930 the name changed to Birds Eye.

The millionaire Birdseyes settled into a new home where they could indulge their passion for horticulture. Bob was interested in hydroponics and believed there was enough growing space on the roofs and in the cellars of New York to feed the whole city with fresh vegetables by this method.

For the Birds Eye company, however, business was an uphill battle. The frozen product might have revolutionised the processing

A Good Idea at the Time
The Ice House

In the UK, where, on average, every person eats around 2.25 kilograms of frozen peas a year, the pea is the nation's favourite vegetable. Freezing farm peas is a stopwatch affair where the grower has precisely 150 minutes to get the peas picked and chilled before they start to deteriorate. But long before Bob Birdseye patented his frosted food process, kitchen gardeners were rushing fresh vegetables to the ice house. Popularised by Charles II, who had an ice house built in St James Park in 1600, the ice house was all the rage among the country set of the 1700s and 1800s.

Built of stone or brick and set in the ground or the side of a hill, the pit of the house was filled with ice cut from some neighbouring lake during the winter. Packed down and kept dry, the ice would keep for twelve months or more. The chamber above the ice was lined with chilled shelves and rails where fresh vegetables and foods were stored until required. But, while the gardeners on estates like Dalmery Park, Dundas Castle and Doddington House were justly proud of their estate ice houses, ice had been used to chill food by the ancient Chinese and, remarkably, the Meso-

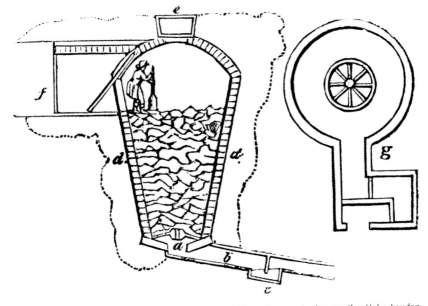

A plan for a nineteenth-century ice house. The ice would keep for over twelve months. (*John Loudon, Encyclopaedia of Gardening*)

potamian gardeners 4,000 years earlier. And Alexander the Great is said to have had trenches dug and filled with mountain snow and covered with branches at Petra so that his soldiers could still enjoy cool wine, fruit and vegetables even in the heat of summer.

An early Birdseye frosted foods store. But many doubted whether freezer foods would ever catch on. (*Birds Eye Foods*)

of fresh vegetables, but storekeepers had to be persuaded to make room for a frozen food cabinet and housewives to add a freezer to their list of desirable white goods. Many housewives were reluctant, not least because they were convinced that 'frosting' vegetables was merely a means of preserving second-grade produce. But they had to concede that 'frosted peas' seemed to taste sweeter than fresh peas. It was true: frosted peas continued to convert starch into sugar even when frozen.

Birds Eye persisted, confident that a food revolution was on the way. Even in the 1930s it predicted that a day would come when the public would buy its food from a central store where butcher, delicatessen, greengrocer and fish shop were amalgamated. Who, asked the food writers, would welcome such a development? And why would anyone want to eat frozen peas at Christmas or 'fresh' fish that was six months old? A glance into any supermarket trolley today tells its own story.

A Vegetable Calendar

FEBRUARY

In the Saxon calendar, February was the month of the cabbage.

2.   An old country saying suggested this was the first day to sow peas, but only if the weather was wet.

9.   Birthday plant of the day is the leek. To eat leeks is to suffer humiliation.

17. Birthday plant is the pea, symbol of respect.

MARCH

1.   St David's Day, when the leek is traditionally worn by Welsh people. St David instructed his brothers to wear a leek when they went into battle against the Saxons.

1.   An old country saying suggests this was the last day to sow peas.

25. Lady Day. Traditional day to pay the first half year's allotment rent.

Ash Wednesday – the traditional day to eat parsnips for those observing Lent.

APRIL

Good Friday – the day to plant potatoes once they have been sprinkled with Holy Water.

MAY
National Asparagus Month in France.

JUNE
11. National Asparagus Festival in France.
13. Birthday plant of the day was the potato, the symbol of benevolence.
21. Time to lift your tree onions.
21. The last day for cutting your asparagus.
21. The arrival of the first crop of peas, 'harbinger of summer', according to Shirley Hibberd.

JULY
25, 26, 27.   The world's biggest garlic festival at Gilroy, California.
26. St Anne's Day and garlic and basil fair at Tours in France.

AUGUST
Annual Potato Festival at Alliston, the potato capital of Ontario.
3rd weekend. Onion Festival, Roscoff, Brittany.

SEPTEMBER
Tomato Festival at Château de la Bourdaisière, Montlouis-sur-Loire, France.
Potimarron (a Japanese squash) Festival at Lunéville, France.
1.   The Saint of Spades day.
19. Birthday plant is the cabbage, symbol of profit and gain.
27. Birthday plant is the dandelion, symbol of bitterness and grief.
29. Michaelmas. Traditional day to pay the second half year's allotment rent.

OCTOBER
2nd Monday in the month. Thanksgiving Day in Canada and pumpkin pie is on the menu.

Halloween – scoop out a pumpkin, set a candle inside to keep out the dead.
31. Birthday plant is the nettle, symbol of spite.

NOVEMBER
Annual display of unusual vegetables at Saint-Jean de Beauregard, France.
4th Thursday in the month. Time to eat pumpkin pie during the US Thanksgiving Day.

DECEMBER
21. Place an onion under your pillow and you will dream the face of your future wife.
The shortest day – the time to plant the tree onion.
22. According to the Roman Columella, early cucumbers could be raised by cutting down the stem of a fennel or bramble and slotting the seed of a cucumber into the pith of the mother plant shortly after the winter equinox.

Further Reading

The vegetable world is filled with wonderful writings from the 1600s onwards. I am indebted to all those authors who have already followed the vegetal trail – and recommend them to any wishing to continue along it.

Adam the Gardener (Sunday Express publications, 1976)

Amos, Sharon, 'Thriving in the Garden', *Country Living* (September 2002)

Baeyer, Edwina von, and Crawford, Pleasance, *Garden Voices: Two Centuries of Canadian Garden Writing* (Random House of Canada, 1997)

Bareham, Lindsey, *In Praise of the Potato* (Grafton Books, 1991)

Barkas, Janet, *The Vegetable Passion* (Routledge, Kegan & Paul, 1975)

Batchelor, John, *There is no Wealth but Life* (Chatto & Windus, 2000)

Beale, Catherine, *Hampton Court: A Brief History* (Hampton Court Estate, 2000)

Berrall, Julia S., *The Garden: An Illustrated History* (Penguin Books, 1978)

Blunt, Wilfred, *The Compleat Naturalist – A Life of Linnaeus* (Frances Lincoln, 2001)

Boff, Charles, *The Big Book of Gardening* (Odhams Press, n.d.)

Briffa, Dr John, 'I Can See Clearly Now', *Observer Magazine*, 25 August 2002

—— 'It Won't End in Tears', *Observer Magazine*, 27 April 2002

Brown, Jane, *The Pursuit of Paradise* (HarperCollins, 1999)

Bunyard, E.A., *The Gardener's Companion* (J.M. Dent, 1936)

Campbell, Susan, *Charleston Kedding* (Ebury Press, 1996)

Carroll, Maureen, 'They Came, they Saw, they Conquered', *The Garden* (RHS Journal, June 2003)

Cobbett, William, *The English Gardener* (1838)

Crouch, David, and Ward, Colin, *The Allotment* (Faber, 1988)

Dannatt, Adrian, 'Undercover Agent', *Guardian*, 7 June 2003

Davies, Jennifer, *The Wartime Kitchen and Garden* (BBC Books, 1993)

Devonshire, Duchess of, *The Garden at Chatsworth* (Frances Lincoln, 1999)

Dickens, Charles, *Dombey and Sons* (Knopf, 1994)

Don, Monty, 'Eat with Beet', *Observer Magazine*, 9 February 2003

Drower, George, *Gardeners, Gurus and Grubs – The Stories of Garden Inventors and Innovations* (Sutton Publishing 2001)

Ducas, Jane, 'The Complete Works of Nature', *Weekend Telegraph*, 15 January 2000

Dudley, Stuart, *Taking the Ache out of Gardening* (The Garden Book Club, 1962)

Dyer, Christopher, *Everyday Life in Medieval England* (Hambledon & London, 1994)

Food, special reports in the *Guardian* (May 2003)

Gardiner, Richard, *Profitable Instructions for the Manuring, Sowing and Planting of Kitchen Gardens* (Edward Allde, 1599)

Garmey, Jane, *The Writer in the Garden* (Chapel Hill, NY, Algonquin Books, 1999)

Green, Candida Lycett, and Lawson, Andrew, *Brilliant Gardens* (Chatto & Windus, 1989)

Griffiths, Mark, *The Times: A Century in Photographs – Gardening* (Times Books, 2000)

Grigson, Jane, *The Vegetable Book* (Michael Joseph, 1978; Penguin Books, 1980)

Guillet, Dominique, *The Seeds of Kokopelli* (Association Kokopelli, 2002)

Hadfield, Miles (ed.), *The Gardener's Companion* (J.M. Dent, 1936)

Hamilton, Geoff, *Successful Organic Gardening* (Dorling Kindersley, 1987)

Hanawalt, B., *The Ties that Bound* (Oxford University Press, 1986)

Hellyer, Arthur, *The Shell Guide to Gardens* (Book Club Associates, 1977)

Hellyer, A.G.L., *The Amateur Gardener* (W.H. & L. Collingridge, 1948)

Hibberd, Shirley, *Profitable Gardening* (Groombridge & Son, n.d.)

Hill, Thomas, *see* Mountain, Didymus

Hills, Lawrence D., *Comfrey, Past Present & Future* (Faber, 1976)

—— *Organic Gardening* (Penguin Books, 1977)

—— *Fighting like the Flowers: The Life Story of Britain's Best-Known Organic Gardener* (Green Books, 1989)

Huxley, Anthony, *An Illustrated History of Gardening* (Paddington Press, 1983)

Jay, Roni, *Sacred Gardens* (Thorsons, 1998)

King, Ronald, *The Quest for Paradise* (Whittet Books, 1979)

Landsberg, Sylvia, *The Medieval Garden* (Thames & Hudson, 1996)

Lawrence, Elizabeth, *Gardening for Love* (Duke University Press, 1987)

Lawrence, W.J.C., *Catch the Tide: Adventures in Horticultural Research* (Grower Books, 1980)

Laws, Bill, *Artists' Gardens* (Ward Lock, 1999)

Loudon, J.C., *An Encyclopaedia of Gardening* (Longman, Rees, Orme, Brown & Green, 1822)

Lovelock, Yann, *The Vegetable Book: An Unnatural History* (George, Allen & Unwin, 1972)

McQuillan, Dan, 'Queen of Spuds', *Sainsbury's Magazine* (October 2002)

Maybe, Richard, *Flora Britannica* (Sinclair-Stevenson, 1996)

Morgan, Joan, and Richards, Alison, *A Paradise out of a Common Field* (Random Century Group, 1990)

Mountain, Didymus (Thomas Hill), *The Gardener's Labyrinth* (1st edn 1577; 2nd edn 1594)

Moynahan, Brian, *The British Century* (Weidenfeld & Nicolson, 1997)

Parkinson, John, *A Garden of Pleasant Flowers* (1st edn 1629; Dover Publications, 1976)

Pears, Pauline (editor in chief), *Encyclopedia of Organic Gardening* (Dorling Kindersley, 2002)

Potter, Beatrix, *The Tale of Peter Rabbit* (F. Warne & Co., 1902)

Pudney, John, *The Smallest Room* (Michael Joseph, 1954)

Rackham, Oliver, *The History of the Countryside* (J.M. Dent, 1986)

Roberts, Jonathon, *Cabbages and King: The Origins of Fruit and Vegetables* (Collins, 2001)

Roddick, Anita, *Take It Personally* (Thorsons, 2001)

Saunders, Nicholas, *Alternative England and Wales* (Nicholas Saunders, 1975)

Seymour, John, *The Complete Book of Self Sufficiency* (Faber & Faber, 1976)

—— and Girardet, Herbert, *Blueprint for a Green Planet* (Dorling Kindersley, 1987)

Sharkey, Olive, *Common Knowledge* (Melbourne, McPhee Gribble Publishers, 1988)

Shephard, Sue, *Pickled, Potted and Canned* (Simon & Schuster, 2000)

Simons, Arthur, *The Vegetable Grower's Handbook* (Penguin Books, 1945)

Smit, Tim, *The Lost Gardens of Heligan: A Brief History and Guide* (Heligan Gardens Ltd, 1992)

—— and McMillan Browse, Philip, *The Heligan Vegetable Bible* (Victor Gollanz, 1988)

Soper, John, *Biodynamic Gardening* (Souvenir Press, 1995)

Spencer, Colin, *The Heretic's Feast: A History of Vegetarianism* (Fourth Estate, 1993)

Steer, William, *Gardening Encyclopaedia* (Spring Books, n.d.)

Strong, Roy, *Royal Gardens* (BBC Books and Conran Octopus, 1992)

Sudell, Richard, *The New Illustrated Gardening Encycolopaedia* (Odhams Press, n.d.)

Talbot, Rob, and Whiteman, Robin, *Brother Cadfael's Herb Garden* (Little, Brown, 1996)

Taylor, Gordon, and Cooper, Guy, *Gardens of Obsession* (Weidenfeld & Nicolson, 1999)

Thoreau, Henry David, *Thoreau: Walden and Other Writings* (Bantam Classic, 1962)

Thunn, Maria, and Thunn, Matthias, *The Sowing and Planting Calendar: Working with the Stars* (Floris Books, 2003)

Tompkins, Peter, and Bird, Christopher, *The Secret Life of Plants* (Allen Lane, 1975)

The Top 10 of Everything (Dorling Kindersley, 1997)

Tucker, David M., *Kitchen Gardening in America* (Iowa State University Press, 1993)

Tusser, Thomas, *Five Hundred Pointes of Good Husbandrie* (1573); repr. as *500 Points of Good Husbandry* (Oxford University Press, 1984)

The Victorian Garden Catalogue (Studio Editions, 1995)

White, Gilbert, *Garden Kalendar* (Scolar Press, 1975)

Whittell, Giles, 'Have Peas had their Chips?', *The Times*, 12 June 2002

Williamson, Tom, and Taigel, Anthea (eds.), *Gardens in Norfolk 1550–1900* (Centre of East Anglian Studies, 1990)

Woodward, Marcus, *Gerard's Herball* (Bracken Books, 1985)

Worlidge, John, *Systema agriculturae* (1669)

Zuckerman, Larry, *The Potato* (Pan, 2000)

Index

Index

Index

Index